The House of Dance & Feathers:

A MUSEUM BY RONALD W. LEWIS

Text by Rachel Breunlin & Ronald W. Lewis

With Essays by
Rachel Breunlin
Helen A. Regis

Neighborhood Story Project
P.O. Box 19742
New Orleans, LA 70179
www.neighborhoodstoryproject.org

Editor: Rachel Breunlin
Consulting Editor: Helen A. Regis
Graphic Designer: Gareth Breunlin

Front cover: A beaded patch sewn by Ronald W. Lewis as part of a Mardi Gras Indian
suit for his son, Rashad Lewis. Photograph by Beverly Kunze. Courtesy of Beverly Kunze Photography.
Back cover: Rashad Lewis wearing the patch on Mardi Gras Day.
Photograph by Ronald W. Lewis

Made Possible Through a Grant from
LOUISIANA
ENDOWMENT
FOR THE
HUMANITIES
State Affiliate of the National Endowment
for the Humanities

ISBN-10: 0-9706190-7-3
ISBN-13: 978-0-9706190-7-5

Library of Congress Control Number: 2009922022

http://unopress.uno.edu

Dedication

To the people of the Lower Ninth Ward,
and all of the survivors of Hurricane Katrina.

Ronald W. Lewis greets the crowd during the Big Nine Social & Pleasure Club's 2008 parade. Photograph by Abram Himelstein.

Acknowledgements

Thank you to everyone who helped make and inspire this book. The list is long and the love behind it is deep.

To Helen Regis for sharing and working on interviews together, talking through ideas, editing for the big and small pictures, tracking down photographs and maps, providing mountains of African art books, and writing two of our introductions.

To the Neighborhood Story Project (NSP) staff: Lindsey Darnell for her work as program coordinator on this book, including all her help in the archives, in the field, and juggling hundreds of to do items; Abram Himelstein for his support even when we were too busy, editorial feedback, and publishing expertise; and Lea Downing for help bringing the book to print.

To Gareth Breunlin for numerous rounds of graphic design and to more than eight years of collaborations—we couldn't do it without you.

To Siobhan McKiernan for her help thinking through captions and copy editing. You professionalize us.

To the University of New Orleans for their ongoing support of the NSP's collaborative ethnographies, particularly Susan Krantz, Joe King, Rick Barton, and the Anthropology Department's David Beriss, Jeffrey Ehrenreich, and Martha Ward. At UNO Press, a big shout out to Bill Lavender and G.K. Darby for their help on the publishing end.

To the Louisiana Endowment for the Humanities for a Public Humanities grant that supported the publication of this catalogue. A special thank you to Erik Charpentier and Walker Lasiter for their patience and encouragement throughout the bookmaking process. To the Lupin Foundation: Your ongoing support allows us to do what we do.

To Sylvester and Anita Francis at the Backstreet Cultural Museum for their ongoing support of the House of Dance & Feathers, and for their generous contributions to the catalogue.

To all the photographers who have contributed images to the collection and supported their publication in the catalogue: Patrick Rhodes, Abram Himelstein, Syndey Byrd, L.J. Goldstein, Eric Waters, Andy Levin, Caitlin Heckathorn, Eric Wittman, Aubrey Edwards, Jason Fedak, Lori Waselchuk, Elliott Hammer, Jeffrey David Ehrenreich, Joyce Taylor, Debbie Flemming Caffrey, Norman Cook, Royce Osborn, and Charles Silver. To others who have donated photographs from their personal collections: Paul Chan, Janice Jacobs, Robert "Big Bob" Starks, Ray "Hatchet" Blazio, Melvin Reed, Peter Alexander, Romeo Bougere, Dorothy Hill, Derrick Magee, Alfred "Bucket" Carter, Byron Hogans, Kenneth "Dice" Dykes, and Joe Spot. Thanks to all the unknown photographers whose images have made the journey from family photo albums to the museum, and now this catalogue.

For donating objects (and stories) to the museum that were highlighted in the catalogue, we'd like to thank J. Kyle Manzay, Ada LeMann, Greyhawk Perkins, Helen Regis, L.J. Goldstein, Arthur and Gina Vigne, Kristyna Filipkova, Lucy Beggs, Herlin Riley, Jr., Darryl Keys, Ann

Marie Coviello, Alphonse "Dowee" Robair, Darryl Preston, Monique Jordan, Aquilla Journee, the Dumaine Gang, and Brian Bush. We'd also like to thank Beverly Kunze Photography and Devin Meyers of Fotos for Humanity (a nonprofit that uses volunteer photography services to help community, non-profit, and cultural groups gain control and benefit from the use of their image) for photographing objects for this publication.

For contributing to stories for our section on the Lower Ninth Ward, we'd like to thank Wayne Hill, Glen David Andrews, Dan Etheridge, Jason Fedak, Patrick Rhodes, Aubrey Edwards, Sarah Gamble, and Dan Baum.

For sharing experiences in the world of Mardi Gras Indians, Social Aid and Pleasure Clubs, and Skeletons, we'd like to thank Ray "Hatchet" Blazio and Franklin "Wingy" Davis of the Wild Apaches; Ronald "Buck" Baham of the Seventh Ward Warriors; Lil Charles and Joyce Taylor of White Cloud Hunters; Victor Harris of Fi Yi Yi; Melvin Reed; Joyce Montana; Tyrone Casby of the Mohawk Hunters; Lil Walter Cook of the Creole Wild West; Issac "Ike" Edwards of the White Eagles; Monk Boudreaux of the Golden Blades; Edgar Jacobs of the Choctaw Hunters; Nelson Burke and Alphonse "Dowee" Robair of Red Hawk Hunters; Romeo Bougere of the Ninth Ward Hunters; Keith "KiKi" Gibson, Darryl Keys, and Percy Francois (and his uncle Keith) of the Comanchee Hunters; Derrick Magee, Alanzo "Harry" Moore, and Terry Carr of the Ninth Ward Navajo; and legendary sewers Ricky Gettridge, Gilbert "Cosmo" Dave, and John Scott.

Robert "Big Bob" Starks of the Big Nine; Richard "Richie Rich" Brown of too many clubs to name; Alfred "Bucket" Carter of the First Division of the Young Men Olympian; Byron Hogans and Gus Lewis of the Dumaine Gang; Monique Jordan, former Queen of the CTC Steppers; Joe Stern of the Prince of Wales; Kenneth "Dice" Dykes and Adrian "Coach Teedy" Gaddies of Sudan; Lois Andrews of the Money Wasters; Phonett Davis; Eric Gardner of Nine Times; Linda Porter and Nicole Wells of the Lady Buck Jumpers; Aquilla Journee of the Popular Ladies; Kevin Dunn of the Original Four; Jack Matranga of the Pennant Shop, Inc.; and Perry Franklin, Gaynelle Butler, and all the members of Keepin It Real at Club Good Times.

In the world of bones, thanks to Chief Al, Acting Chief Bruce "Sunpie" Barnes, and Royce Osborn of the North Side Skull and Bones Gang, and Derek Meilleur.

And to all the other Indian gangs, clubs, second liners, and Mardi Gras maskers whose presence has made this catalogue richer.

We'd like to thank the following archives in Louisiana: Irene Wainwright at the New Orleans Public Library, Louisiana Division, City Archives & Special Collections; Brenda Square at the Amistad Research Center; Daniel Hammer (for going above and beyond what was reasonable) and Jude Solomon at the Historic New Orleans Collection; Lynn Abbott and Bruce Boyd Raeburn at The William Ransom Hogan Archive of New Orleans Jazz; Florence M. Jumonville at the Louisiana & Special Collections Department, Earl K. Long Library, University of New Orleans; and Nancy Burris and Lynn Cunningham at *The Times-Picayune*.

For help finding images to represent American Indian beading and war bonnets: Jack Heriard at Written Heritage; Rev. Raymond A. Bucko, S.J., at the Buechel Memorial Lakota Museum, St. Francis Mission; Elena and Mercedes Whitecloud; Joyce Growing Thunder and Juanita Growing Thunder; and Paul Tarver at the New Orleans Museum of Art.

For help with Day of the Dead images, thanks to Joyce Bishop and to Emily Socolov at Mano a Mano: Mexican Culture Without Borders.

For help with Yoruba beadwork, thanks to African art historian Henry John Drewal. For help with Haitian sequin arts, much thanks to Tina Girouard and Anthony Fisher at Indigo Arts Gallery. For cross cultural images of parades: Elizabeth McAlister, Chantal Regnault, Herbert "Skip" Cole, and Jacques Morial.

For editorial feedback and literature recommendations, thanks to Rachel's reading group: Matt Sakakeeny, Rebecca Snedecker, Bethany Rogers, and Chris Jones. For help thinking about framing the book, thanks to Ronald "Buck" Baham, Nelia Dias, Royce Osborn, and Bill Fagaly.

To our boards. At the House of Dance & Feathers: Helen Regis, L.J. Goldstein, and Dan Etheridge. At the NSP: Bob Cashner, Susan Krantz, Corlita Mahr, Troy Materre, Helen Regis, Petrice Sams-Abiodun, and Emelda Wylie.

To all the people who have contributed their time, energy, and money to support the House of Dance & Feathers, especially the team that rebuilt the museum. At Project Locus: Patrick Rhodes, Jerryn McCray, and Jorge Marien.

At Kansas State: Larry Bowne, Jennifer Howe, Nathan Howe, Gary Coates, Todd Gabbard, John Selfridge, Dragoslav Simic, David Sachs, and Jim Middlebrook. And students in the architecture department: Scott Capps, Brian Copeland, Jason Fedak, Caitlin Heckathorn, Clemente Jaquez-Herrera, Melody Jacobson, Kyle Wedel, Eric Wittman, Sally Maddock, Scott Newland, Annette Rice, Aaron Schump, Carrie Steins,

Adrienne Stolwyk, Joe Vessel, Jessica Williams, Brent Hansen, and Andrew Hiemberger.

In Missoula, Montana: Robin Saha, Tom Roy, Len Broberg, students in the Environmental Studies Department at University of Montana, Melissa Arno and youth from Tom Roy Guidance Home, and Susan O'Connor.

From other schools and fellowships around the country: Noah Cahan, Lucy Begg, Kristyna Filipkova, Tomas Martinek, Justin Mullins, JoEllen Wang, Jared Hueter, and the Manhattan Area Vo-Tech Welding Department.

Many other individuals who have made a lasting contribution to the museum, including Cliff Wright, Charles "Yacky" Napoleon, Demetrius Alexander, Ben Gauslin, Carol Mockbee, Wes Chambers, Jennifer Hardy, and Barry Downing, and Joyce Marie Jackson.

To all the organizations, foundations, businesses, and individuals who helped to fund the rebuild and continue to support the museum, including the Charles Engelhard Foundation for its generous donation, which enabled the project to happen, as well as the 6t'9 Social Aid & Pleasure Club, Arkansas School of Architecture, CITYbuild, the Green Project, the Tulane City Center, Habitat ReStore, and ACORN. Thanks to the Annenberg Foundation for ongoing operational support, and to Bryan Bell and Design Corps for structural support, including fiscal sponsorship.

Finally and always, to our families: Rebecca Wright Dickerson, Charlotte Hill Lewis, Ronaldo and Rashad Lewis, the Hill-Lastie-Andrews clan, and the rest of the Lewis family; Michael, Maria, and Lauren Darnell; and Dan Etheridge and the little one whose presence became stronger and stronger during the making of this book—we can't wait to meet you.

Table of Contents

Opposite page and following spread: The House of Dance & Feathers. Photographs by Patrick Rhodes.

Part I

Ronald W. Lewis holding a beaded patch he sewed for his son Rashad's Mardi Gras Indian suit. Photography by Devin Meyers of Fotos for Humanity.

Introduction

Ronald W. Lewis displays some of his photographs from the House of Dance & Feathers at the New Orleans Jazz & Heritage Festival.

The Making of a Museum and Its Catalogue

By Rachel Breunlin and Ronald W. Lewis

Ronald W. Lewis: When you see there's something missing in your community, you want to contribute to make it whole. I thought cultural education was the missing part in the Lower Ninth Ward of New Orleans, and I've worked to create a museum to help fill in this blank.

The House of Dance & Feathers has been a fixture in the Lower Ninth Ward since 2003. It's located in my backyard on Tupelo Street. I've lived there for 30 years, and it's always been a central place of being—from the time when my boys were growing up with their friends, building clubhouses with a yard full of bicycles. Before Hurricane Katrina, the building was a museum, but it was also a barbershop and the grandchildren's playhouse.

Rachel Breunlin: I first heard about the House of Dance & Feathers a few months after the storm, when Ronald and I participated in a rebuilding

workshop called *ReInhabiting NOLA*. My husband, Dan Etheridge, had spent months planning it. Like many residents of the city, we had returned home manic, overwhelmed, and wanting to help reclaim our neighborhoods again.

Ronald drove in from Lafourche Parish, just south of the city. Unable to return to the Lower Ninth Ward, he was living in Thibodaux and working on a documentary project about his family history and exile. During the conference, he passed around a photo album of black and white pictures that he had taken. Many of the people he had photographed at "Camp Stopher," a shelter in Thibodaux, were from his neighborhood. It reminded me of the mission of the Neighborhood Story Project: Our stories told by us.

Ronald: I photographed a lot in New Orleans and always thought I was the master of the ten-dollar camera. While I was in exile, I found out that documentary work was my destiny. Before Katrina it was just something for me to do, but here, it was a true passion of really getting something done.

Rachel: In the months that followed, I got to know Ronald as Dan helped put together a team to rebuild the House of Dance & Feathers. While plans were being put into place for the reconstruction, a mutual friend, Helen Regis, began to record Ronald's stories around his Thibodaux documentary. We talked about the Neighborhood Story Project publishing the work, but as the museum came back to life and served as an important resource in the Lower Ninth Ward, it became

we used his exhibits and archives to build our primary narratives, but translated his tours and informal history lessons into text as well. When Ronald walks visitors through the museum, he weaves his personal stories into the story of the community. Every visit is different because he encourages a dialogue with his guests.

New Orleans Street Culture

The foundation of Ronald's museum is based on his participation in the street cultures of New Orleans, which include a network of grassroots, working class African American organizations

Left: Big Chief Edgar Jacobs and the Choctaw Hunters Mardi Gras Indian tribe's second line. Photograph donated by Edgar's wife, Janice Jacobs [*walking behind Edgar on right with sunglasses*]. *Right:* Dwayne Taylor, Little Joseph, and Jonas Tyler before a Big Nine Social & Pleasure Club parade. Designer Robert "Big Bob" Starks was inspired by the canes decorated with carnations carried by members of the St. Patrick and St. Joseph Day parades in New Orleans. To make them, Big Bob took umbrellas, built foam around them, inserted the flowers, and then hot glued the stems to keep them in place. The ribbons hanging down say, "Big 9 S & P Club." Photograph donated by Big Bob.

clear that a more holistic story deserved to be told. We wanted to place the story of Katrina and exile into the larger story of his community.

After a number of brainstorming meetings, we decided to create a book where Ronald could tell the story of how he became a self-taught photographer, archivist, curator, and cultural translator. As he began to put his collection back together,

called Mardi Gras Indians and social aid and pleasure clubs.[1] As he became more involved in these communities, Ronald transformed his house on Tupelo Street into a workshop where he worked on regalia for Mardi Gras day or Sunday afternoon second line parades. Over the years, his family's modest cottage started to resemble a storage space.

Ronald: I was working on my Mardi Gras Indian costumes for the Choctaw Hunters, a Mardi Gras Indian tribe I helped start in the Lower Ninth Ward. While I was working on the suits, I had feathers and memorabilia all over the house. I came home one day and everything was in my backyard. My loving wife, Charlotte (who we call Minnie), said, "I can't take this any more. You've got to find something to do with this." I moved the artwork into the shed, renovated it into a building with my sons, and started putting up my various artifacts. The children in the community started calling it a museum and I gave it a name, "The House of Dance & Feathers," which means second lining and Mardi Gras Indians.

I was at the point in my life where, "Okay. I can make a Mardi Gras Indian costume, but I want to educate the world about our great culture, how we do this, and why we are so successful at it even though the economics say we ain't supposed to be." For years, I had heard people label us "poor blacks" because our economics don't fit into the status quo. People come to New Orleans, and the first thing they want to signify is our economics instead of looking at our creativity.[2]

Rachel: When I was in my early 20s, I came to know this creativity for the first time. In my mostly white, middle class family, we watched parades, went to galleries and museums, and passed down knowledge through books and conversation. While our doors were open to friends from all over the world, we didn't communicate through dance, and music was barely a backdrop. At my first second line in New Orleans, I watched from the sidewalk until a stranger told me I needed to jump off the curb and into the crowd. How else would I keep up with the band? I couldn't believe I was worthy of the invitation—that I could be part of the art on the street.

Many years and parades later, while I was supervising a project in the Seventh Ward for one of my students in the Neighborhood Story Project, I received another invitation. Ronald "Buck" Baham, the Big Chief of the Seventh Ward Warriors, told me to stop by his house the night before Mardi Gras. He had worked for three years on the suit he planned to wear the next day, and people from all over the Seventh Ward were crowded in half a shotgun double to see the final touches.

Kyle Lacoste "playing Indian" with Leroy Ross, Flagboy of the White Cloud Hunters, at Ronald "Buck" Baham's house in the Seventh Ward on Lundi Gras 2005. Mardi Gras Indians from the White Cloud Hunters and Black Feather showed him how to signal he's a Spyboy by mimicking binoculars. Buck says, "I organized it. He didn't know it was going to happen. I just wanted him to have fun so he wouldn't be afraid. It's a thing of beauty." Photographs by Rachel Breunlin.

It was also the first year that his Spyboy, Kyle Lacoste, was going to mask. Deep into the night, I overheard Buck tell some of the other Indians that he wanted them to teach him how to dance. I imagined Kyle being taken aside and shown the

Left: In the 1940s, a painter named Homer E. Turner took photographs of Mardi Gras Indians, primarily for his personal collection. Photograph courtesy of the Historic New Orleans Collection *Right:* Artist Ralston Crawford photographed the Jolly Bunch Social & Pleasure Club in the 1950s, when he needed a police permit to enter a Black club as a white man.[4] Photograph courtesy of the Ralston Crawford Collection of Jazz Photography, Hogan Jazz Archive, Tulane University.

steps, but as the hours passed and people mingled, sang Indian songs, and helped hook up the beaded patches to the rest of the suits, it seemed the lesson had been forgotten.

And then there was a shout at the front door. Leroy Ross called out, "SPYBOY!" Kyle stood in the living room and Buck told him, "You better answer him." We all turned towards him, waiting for his response. I worried he might be too shy, but he was up for the challenge, and hollered out a greeting, "Spyboy, Seventh Ward Warriors! Coochie molly!" One by one, other Indians stepped forward and called to him, and Kyle answered them all until he was told he did good. He didn't bow down. A repertoire of song and dance had passed down from one generation to the next.[3]

Outside Representation

I loved this moment and held it close to my heart throughout the rest of the semester as I taught school and worked on books. I had taken some pictures, and went back to Buck's house to give him copies as a thank you for letting me be a part of the night.

As I sat in his living room, something shifted in my bag and there was a clicking sound, like a tape recorder shutting off. Buck, usually easygoing, jumped up. Was I secretly taping our conversation? I told him, No, you can check to see if you want. I can still remember blushing as I confronted my naive belief that I was outside the larger, complicated history of documentary work in New Orleans.

Buck said he believed me, but we were still caught in this history, unsure how to move on. And then he said, "I'd like to interview *you*." His questions about what led me to help people write their own books about New Orleans leveled the playing field and were the beginning of a friendship and collaboration that's grown over the last five years.

When I began working on this project with Ronald, I was mindful of all of the converations I've had with Buck. Similar points were made by other Mardi Gras Indians we spoke to while working on the catalogue. One of Ronald's good friends, Ray Blazio, Big Chief of the Wild Apaches, explained the skepticism from within the performance traditions, "A lot of them came around with that education—PhDs and stuff—and stole a lot. They're just repeating what they done heard and using the extravagant words. They never masked, but people be believing what they say."[5]

Any time you go to a Sunday afternoon parade or hang out on LaSalle and Washington during carnival, you are likely to run into photographers, filmmakers, and scholars documenting the events. The phenomenon isn't new. Since the 1940s, there has been an interest in the

Left: Richard "Ivory" Turner made a name for himself running Wildman for the Ninth Ward Hunters. Unlike most Wildman suits, which tended to have a shirt with no sleeves, fur, and perhaps one or two patches, Ivory's suits were more like a flagboy suit with horns. His crown was particularly unique—the feathers went straight back into a mohawk with horns sticking out on either side. Over the years, a rivalry developed between Ivory and the Creole Wild West's Malcom "Wildman Mackey" Williams, who was also a great sewer. Some of these suits were documented in Michael Smith's 1994 book *Mardi Gras Indians.* The Turner family, based in the Lower Ninth Ward, lost all of their photographs of Ivory during Hurricane Katrina, and Smith's collection is one of the only places where they know images exist. Photograph of Ivory by Michael P. Smith, courtesy of the Historic New Orleans Collection. *Right:* Taken in the mid-1990s at a large Mardi Gras Indian gathering near Shakespeare Park called Super Sunday, the frame expands beyond the Mardi Gras Indians to include the surrounding scene with the documenters. Here we see three pairs: a mother holding her small child, a Mardi Gras Indian dancing with a little boy, and a photographer with her camera. Photograph by L.J. Goldstein.

processions, but over the years the number of documentary projects has grown. In his book *Mardi Gras Indians,* Michael P. Smith brings up some of the issues that arise:

> A cherished activity, essentially a religious activity, pursued in private spaces and isolated neighborhoods for more than a century, has been thrown into a strange new public marketplace. Art collectors, record producers, music managers, and other entrepreneurs see the Indian gangs as an economic opportunity...Especially confusing is the "role" of outside documentarians and folklorists (black and white) who now frequent the community. How does one distinguish between fellow artists and supporters, and commercial entrepreneurs who take and run, giving nothing back to the community?[6]

Smith was a documentary photographer whose work on New Orleans African American street performances has been the source of a great deal of recognition and controversy. Although Smith had spent many years with the subjects of his photographs, and had written directly about the issue of what he calls "the third line"—the documenters who follow second lines—many Mardi Gras Indians represented in his book were upset that they weren't consulted before their images were published. Many also have a copy of the book in their own archives. In the years since Smith's publication, other publications, exhibitions, and talks at institutions such as the New Orleans Jazz & Heritage Festival, the Louisiana State Museum, the New Orleans Museum of Art, and the Louisiana Endowment for the Humanities have further developed the dialogue around representation.[7]

If one of the primary goals of street performances is to represent the best of your artistic abilities and to gain recognition for your community, then it is inevitable that as the traditions are represented in other venues, people will want to shape the visual and written depictions of their work. Ronald's museum comes out of a small but growing movement in New Orleans of people "in the culture" creating their own forums to narrate the histories of their traditions and represent their visual power.[8] The Mardi Gras Indian Hall of Fame, an annual awards ceremony organized by Cherice Harrison-Nelson and Roslyn J. Smith, recognizes individuals who have made contributions to the community. The Backstreet Cultural Museum, located in Tremé, serves both visitors and the people involved in the performance traditions.

Magnets for the Community

Ronald: I really credit Sylvester Francis of the Backstreet for having a place we could call our own. He has a great museum with elaborate costumes dedicated to African American parading traditions in New Orleans. We have very few in our culture that brought it to this level. Even though we have the state museums and art galleries that show the history of the culture, they don't carry the same significance as someone who has lived the culture.

As I was nearing my retirement, I started going by the Backstreet Museum, hanging out. Sylvester opened the door for me. When he had a large tour group, he would do the Mardi Gras Indians, his wife, Anita, would do the jazz funeral part, and he would tell me to do the story of the social and pleasure clubs. Sometimes, when he was too busy, I would do the whole program. Not for a monetary reward. He entrusted his livelihood to me. If you're ever around us, you'll hear me call him "Boss Man," cause he was a boss to me.

The Backstreet is a magnet of the community. You could go there at any time and find the who's who of the Mardi Gras Indian or musical community sitting on the porch, sharing special moments. And that's what I envisioned in the Lower Ninth Ward. With no apprehension, Sylvester helped

Top: Sylvester Francis with Mardi Gras Indian costumes from Fi Yi Yi and the Mandingo Warriors at his museum. Reflecting on the importance of his museum, he says, "I think life thrives on the past. Black people's past was so hard that...every chance to express [the good parts] with the community means so much to them...You take the past, the different struggles we done had...to create something [that] can affect our world for years to come...A musuem like this really tells the story—past, present, and future." [9] Photograph by Syndey Byrd, courtesy of the Backstreet Museum. *Center:* Sylvester Francis and Ronald W. Lewis in front of the Backstreet. *Bottom:* Wesley Phillips, Victor Harris, and Jackson Robertson of Fi Yi Yi at their display at the New Orleans Jazz & Heritage Festival. Photograph by Ronald W. Lewis.

Brene Taylor and Reshad Lewis inside the original House of Dance & Feathers. Photograph by Ronald W. Lewis.

me move the House of Dance & Feathers forward. The museum became official in 2005 when I got my papers of incorporation.

Rachel: A few months later, the city called a mandatory evacuation for Hurricane Katrina. Ronald didn't have room in his car to take everything in the museum, but he packed suitcases of photo albums, beaded patches from Indian suits, videos, and framed images. The rest of the collection was flooded in the storm. After weeks in murky storm water, most was unsalvagable. Since the rebuilding of the museum in the summer of 2006, however, the collection has grown.

These days, all of the space in the one-room museum has been claimed. Some objects are handmade, irreplaceable works of art, while others, such as statues of jazz musicians and Indians, dreamcatchers, and ships found at the Dollar Store or at a rest stop alongside the highway, are part of a mass-produced Americana. Some are donated by friends and family, while others may come from the many years he's shared space with other "culture bearers" at the New Orleans

Jazz & Heritage Festival's Folklife Village. Most objects are not labeled, but are artfully arranged to help illustrate the stories Ronald tells in his tours. In addition to the objects, Ronald has taken hundreds of photographs.

Ronald: One of the greatest things I learned from the Mardi Gras Indian culture was to get to know a person out of that costume. Get to know him as an individual. When you see a photo of mine, I usually know the stories behind the suits. It's the same with the parade photos—I could tell you about each club. Over the years, I wanted to know the people, not just the parade. The organizations. Who was the president. We got to know each other on a personal basis, and this is how I try to run my museum, too. I get to know the photographers and the people in the pictures.

Rachel: As the museum has become more established, Ronald asked Indian gangs, S&P clubs, and professional photographers to donate images. The mixture of snapshots, documentary and fine art prints shows alternative visions of the events.[10] The image will be framed differently depending, for instance, on whether the person behind the camera is a cousin or neighbor taking a photograph as you would before any important event—like weddings or a prom—or a visual anthropologist like Jeffrey David Ehrenreich. Before moving to New Orleans, Jeffrey's research had focused, among other things, on

"Squirky Man" Hunter does an aerial straddle in the middle of a second line parade. The photograph was taken by Eric Waters in the early 1990s. Eric explains his decision to donate some of his photographs to the museum: "I would always see Ronald at second lines or the Backstreet. Post-Katrina, he told me to come down and see his museum. I was amazed at what he was doing and told him it would be an honor to contribute. I just want to be able to help with what he and Sylvester are doing. It's very important. I don't think the cultural elite have respect for the Mardi Gras Indian and second line culture because it's a Black thing, yet they utilize it whenever they need to promote the city."

Amazonia, shamanism, the anthropology of the body, and race. Photographing Mardi Gras Indians became an extension of these interests. Jeffrey explains:

> Mardi Gras Indian gangs' tradition is driven by a spiritual connection that relates to shamanic practice around the world. Their use of body display and ornamentation is a classic and thrilling example of the idea of "the body as social text." Their music, art, and social activities are all responses, in one way or another, to the racist conditions and ordeals of the Black experience in America. My photography is done with all of this in mind. I make it available whenever possible to the people who inhabit the pictures. In a sense, the photographs

I take are my payback to the gift and privilege of being permitted to take the photographs in the first place.

Reciprocity is an important ongoing dialogue in the world of street performances. Jeffrey recognizes that his work and relationships are deepened when the photographs are "returned" to the subjects. Giving images to community-based archives like the Backstreet and the House of Dance & Feathers means they will also enter a public sphere that is visited by both people intimately involved in the traditions and those just learning about them for the first time. As the subjects of photographs stop by to visit, the displayed images spark memories, which Ronald may later incorporate into stories he tells during his tours. Of course, the photographers play a role in shaping these histories, too, as their images lead the

9

* Good Fellas
* Big 9
* CTC Steppers
* Keep 'N It Real
* Revolution
2007 - 2008

Richard "Richie Rich" Brown is well known in the second line scene for breaking the record for parading with the most social and pleasure clubs in one year. A lifelong resident of the Ninth Ward, raised in the Desire Projects and on Alabo Street, Richie Rich worked for 21 years as a longshoreman, and now runs Danielle's New Orleans Style Snoballs with his wife. He said all the extra work of actually being a member of all of the clubs is worth it: "When you're dressed up, dancing in the street, everybody's focused on you." The House of Dance & Feathers serves as another venue to highlight his achievement. Photograph donated by Richie Rich. The graphic design and photography were put together by "Nick's Gallery," which is run by a second line photographer who takes pictures at parades and sells them to club members.

particularly in Africa and the African diaspora. In part, this growing interest has developed from conversations with visitors from the Caribbean and beyond who recognize similarities in the performance traditions from their own cultures.[11]

Ronald: My main statement is I'm an African American from New Orleans, but I wanted to put things in here that people outside of New Orleans could relate to as well. Through the masks, through the figures, books, and images, I can have other conversation pieces in here that expand the museum and challenge people to consider who they are connected to.

Rachel: One of the ways that Ronald builds more cross-cultural connections is by asking people who visit his museum to contribute something from their own backgrounds and collections. Others are inspired by their visit and send him donations they think will enrich the museum. This eclectic approach has expanded the museum to include a homemade Garifuna drum, West African masks, and a drum from a member of the United Houma Nation. These layers bend time away from linear narratives of the Lower Ninth Ward and Black cultural traditions in New Orleans.

Other relationships develop into more than a one—time donation. Ronald's long friendship with L.J. Goldstein grew through a cross—cultural exchange in parades. Their collaborations on the street and in the museum have led to many donated objects. L.J.'s satirical Mardi Gras krewe, Krewe du Jieux, was inspired in part by his involvement in social and pleasure clubs, which began as a photographer and then expanded as he became an honorary member of the Happy House and began to parade with the Tremé Sidewalk Steppers.

viewer to see aspects of an event that they may not have noticed before.

Cross—Cultural Connections

More and more, Ronald is also interested in making links between the Black cultural traditions of New Orleans and other cultural groups,

Top right: A mask from the Ivory Coast bought by the actor J. Kyle Manzay in a market in New York City, and donated to the museum when he performed in Paul Chan's production of Samuel Becket's *Waiting for Godot* in the Lower Ninth Ward in November of 2007. *Bottom right:* A postcard from Cameroon sent to Ronald by cultural anthropologist Helen Regis. *Bottom left:* A drum donated by musician and member of the Houma Nation, Greyhawk Perkins, after speaking with Ronald at the New Orleans Jazz & Heritage Festival about their common roots around Thibodaux.

Top left: A Garifuna drum commissioned by Ada LaMann in support of Ronald's commitment to telling the stories of the historical connections between indigenous and African people in the Americas. Ada says, "Ronald's museum is about the preservation of culture—the history of the Mardi Gras Indians. I said, 'I'm interested in preserving my culture as well.'" The Garifuna are of African and Arawak Indian descent. They were relocated from St. Vincent to the Caribbean coast of Central America, and some have since migrated to Louisiana.[12] Ada says, "There's something about a drum that's spiritual—the ancestors are calling you." This drum was made in Dangriga Town, Belize, by a Garifuna craftsman. Photographs by Devin Meyers of Fotos for Humanity.

Ronald: L.J. started on our side of the fence and learned the discipline of how we run social aid and pleasure clubs. He then brought it into another world of Mardi Gras krewes. I mentored him. He showed me another world within the Jewish community and I met some great people. And I tried to fine tune him about our culture and history cause he's in the mode of a son.

After Katrina 2006, Krewe du Jieux marched as the Wandering Jews. Like the rest of the group, I wore glasses with a big nose and a big old Star of David on my back. During the parade, I got cussed by a white man. I looked him in the face. He said, "What you doing with that goddamn Star of David on your back?" He just didn't add the N word to it, but I already felt that. I looked at him for a minute. How could I answer him? I told him, "Look at my nose, motherfucker." He got infuriated and walked off down the street hollering, screaming and cussing. And I went on my way.

When I told L.J. the story I said, "Look at me. Look at the color of my skin. Look at where I grew up in the Deep South. Whether it's anti-Semitism or just the plain old racism, I know about this. So big deal."

What L.J.'s doing is what his people did before him. During the Civil Rights movement, the Jewish people came to the aid of the Blacks in their struggle. They built the bridge of support— technically, physically, mentally they did so. So what he's doing is not nothing new, except for the venue that he's doing it in—parades.

Ronald often credits L.J. for teaching him about black and white photography. He asked L.J. to donate this photograph to the museum. For Ronald, it symbolizes power. L.J. explains that he took the image at an Orthodox Jewish wedding in New Orleans. It's a tradition to raise the bride and groom up on chairs as part of the celebration. On this occasion, they raised the groom up on a table. Photograph of the image on display at the museum by Devin Meyers of Fotos for Humanity.

Rachel: Entering the museum, items from the Jewish and African American cross-cultural parades are on display with other exhibits that focus on American Indian and Pan-African connections. Each time I visit the space, I feel like I am moving into a surreal landscape built on the layering of gift exchange, oral history, and the juxtaposition of objects and images that represent connections between times and places.

Ronald: In my exhibit about Pan–Africanism, I decided to use boats and masks and figurines to show connections across places. The masks represent West African culture and the boats represent those slave ships that brought us to and fro—mostly to. And in the middle, I put an Aunt Jemima doll with its image of racism.

It's easy to just push history to the side, but I don't want to do that because it's there. To be fair, I want to identify with it all. When I talk about my mama coming off that sugarcane plantation, I'm not ashamed of that because that's where my roots are. As I was growing up, my mama always had her hair tied up in a scarf. When I see this doll, I remember that, too, and think about how my family survived those cane fields.

Rachel: Ronald's assemblage provokes the viewer to feel the tensions that exist amongst these different elements. They aren't presented as straightforward narratives, and they aren't easily resolved. They make me think of a chapter in *Freedom Dreams*, where Robin D.G. Kelley talks about how surrealism fits into the black radical imagination. For him, its goal is to "lessen and eventually to completely resolve the contradiction between everyday life and our wildest dreams." [13] As a whole, the House of Dance & Feathers can be viewed one of these in–between spaces.

Exhibit on Pan–Africanism curated by Ronald W. Lewis. Photograph by Devin Meyers of Fotos for Humanity.

From a Physical Space to a Catalogue

As we began to think about the aesthetics of the museum—the assemblages and collages—we recognized that a a strict "catalogue" would go against the spirit of Ronald's work. Instead of documenting the physical characteristics of the objects, Ronald and I were interested in documenting the relationships behind the objects, the process of making the art, and why and how the art is used in practice.

In between a steady stream of visitors, we spent hours going through his collection—framed images, photo albums, and objects—and recording conversations about them. The small space doesn't have air–conditioning, and the only relief from New Orleans' seemingly eternal summer was a large industrial fan. I didn't like turning it on when we were recording stories, but Ronald wasn't flexible on this point. He wasn't going to melt in the name of a clean transcript.

The book continued to take shape through many rounds of edits at the Neighborhood Story Project's writing workshop and in the bay window of my Seventh Ward home. I transcribed and edited our talks, matched stories with images, and, when I got to a stopping point, went back to the museum to talk over the progress with Ronald. One of the initial narratives we wanted to work on was Ronald's story of the Lower Ninth Ward. Combing through the archive, the clubs, Indian gangs, and musicians that call the Lower Nine home could easily have been the sole focus of the book. Ronald was adamant, however, that the book should reflect the larger mission of the museum.

Ronald: The culture is beyond just my community of the Lower Ninth Ward: It's about the whole city of New Orleans. The Indian and parading culture tie different parts of the city together.

Rachel: Consequently, the book has multiple narratives running through it. There is one section dedicated to the Lower Nine, followed by three devoted to the three main collections in the museum: Mardi Gras Indians, Social Aid & Pleasure Clubs, and Skeletons. The narrative of these collections loosely follows Ronald's own involvement in the performance traditions— from learning to sew Indian suits when he was in middle school to helping create a Mardi Gras Indian tribe in the Lower Ninth Ward, to moving into the world of second line parades, and finally, to becoming a member of the North Side Skull and Bones Gang after his retirement. In keeping with the timeline of Ronald's life, the Mardi Gras Indian section reflects more than 40 years of experience, while his direct involvement

in social and pleasure clubs and skull and bones has been more recent, and not as all-consuming.

After we had a rough draft of the text and images we planned to use, my research assistant, Lindsey Darnell, and I spent months talking with the Mardi Gras Indian tribes, social and pleasure clubs, members of bone gangs, photographers, and volunteers involved in the rebuilding of the museum who were represented in the book. As people looked at images connected to particular moments in their lives, they shared other memories and explanations of events that enriched Ronald's narratives about the collection.[14] To honor these contributions, I included extended captions that tell the stories behind the photographs. The final product is closer to a community history—certainly not a definitive one, but one that explores the creative and social lineages that span across the city.

The captions also provide information about the countless photographers and collectors who have made contributions to the museum. Unless otherwise specified, the photographs and objects are a part of the House of Dance & Feathers' collection. In the cases where photographs were donated by someone other than the photographer, all reasonable efforts were made to track down appropriate credit. Unfortunately, as many came from family photo albums or were passed through multiple hands before reaching the museum, the photographer's identity sometimes remains a mystery.

Finally, we have included introductory essays to each of the sections to provide a larger historical and cross-cultural context. Helen Regis contributed two of the essays. After helping to spearhead the rebuild of the museum and to envision

Gilbert "Cosmo" Dave and Ronald work on parade regalia at the House of Dance & Feathers for the Big Nine Social & Pleasure Club's 2008 second line. Written on their fans is the refrain from Barack Obama's election night speech, "Yes We Can." Photograph by Rachel Breunlin.

this project, she was also our main editorial sounding board.

Just as a visit to the museum couldn't replace an experience of actually being in a second line parade, so this book can't replace the experience of being in the museum with Ronald. It is, however, its own kind of cultural artifact. We imagine our readers sitting in a barroom in the Seventh Ward, a café in Des Moines, Iowa, or a cultural center in Santiago de Cuba. We hope that the book will travel, further the cross—cultural links, and provoke debates about histories,

genealogies, and the repatriation of photography. We also hope to inspire literature that is a part of, rather than separate from, the communities it represents.

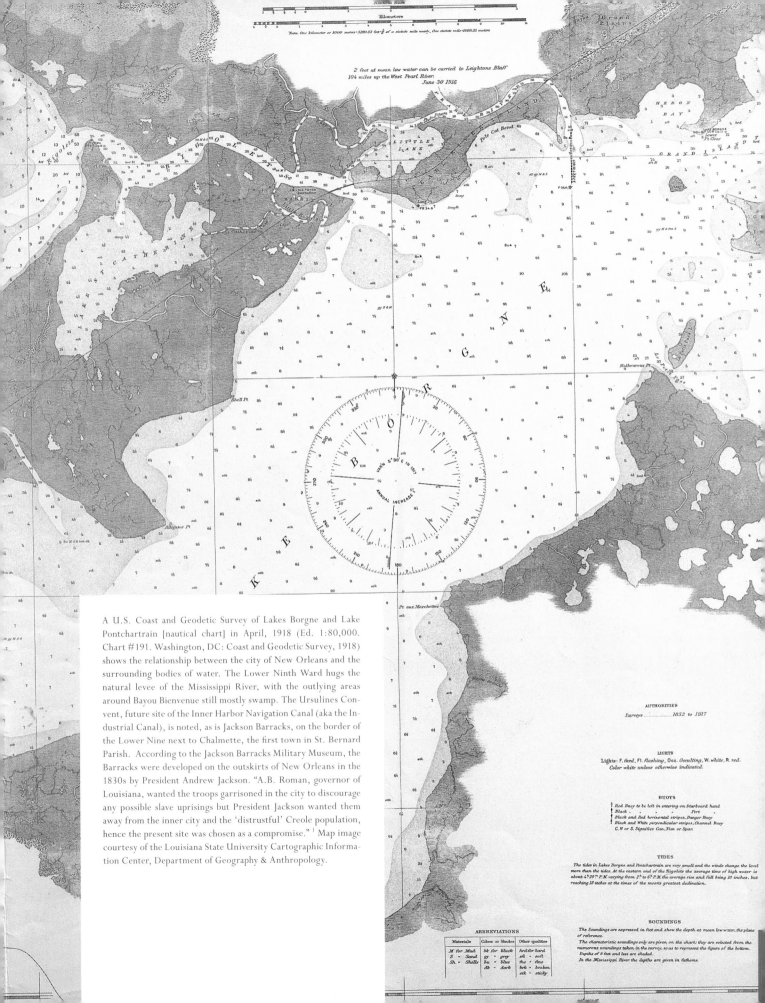

A U.S. Coast and Geodetic Survey of Lakes Borgne and Lake Pontchartrain [nautical chart] in April, 1918 (Ed. 1:80,000. Chart #191. Washington, DC: Coast and Geodetic Survey, 1918) shows the relationship between the city of New Orleans and the surrounding bodies of water. The Lower Ninth Ward hugs the natural levee of the Mississippi River, with the outlying areas around Bayou Bienvenue still mostly swamp. The Ursulines Convent, future site of the Inner Harbor Navigation Canal (aka the Industrial Canal), is noted, as is Jackson Barracks, on the border of the Lower Nine next to Chalmette, the first town in St. Bernard Parish. According to the Jackson Barracks Military Museum, the Barracks were developed on the outskirts of New Orleans in the 1830s by President Andrew Jackson. "A.B. Roman, governor of Louisiana, wanted the troops garrisoned in the city to discourage any possible slave uprisings but President Jackson wanted them away from the inner city and the 'distrustful' Creole population, hence the present site was chosen as a compromise." [1] Map image courtesy of the Louisiana State University Cartographic Information Center, Department of Geography & Anthropology.

Part II

The Lower Ninth Ward after Katrina, in the area between North Claiborne and the Florida Avenue Canal. Photograph by Helen Regis.

In this U.S. Geological Survey of New Orleans and Vicinity, LA (1:24,000. Washington, DC: US Geological Survey, 1951), the Lower Ninth Ward is located on the downriver side of the Industrial Canal. The Intercoastal Navigational Canal runs into the Industrial Canal just a short distance away from the neighborhood. Since the map was created, swampland around the Lower Nine, marked in green, has slowly eroded due to saltwater intrusion from the canals. Map image courtesy of the Louisiana State University Cartographic Information Center, Department of Geography & Anthropology.

"Until recently, not too many people around the world, or around the nation, had heard of the New Orleans neighborhood where I grew up. As a matter of fact, not many in Louisiana or the Crescent City could find their way to the Lower Ninth Ward if they were forced to do so."
—Will Sutton[2]

"But at this place, at this moment of time, all mankind is us, whether we like it or not. Let us make the most of it, before it is too late! Let us represent worthily for once the foul brood to which a cruel fate consigned us! What do you say?"
—Samuel Beckett[3]

INTRODUCTION

Locating the Lower Ninth Ward
By Rachel Breunlin

Ronald's neighborhood, the the Lower Ninth Ward, sits on the edge of New Orleans next to St. Bernard Parish. On the margins of the city for most of its existence, it was on the periphery of official New Orleans history as well. Important community events were often neglected by the press, and the stories and photographs passed down amongst families and neighborhood organizations rarely found their way into books, archives, or museums.

Since Hurricane Katrina, the neighborhood has seen a surge of interest, but as city planners,

activists, and documentarians who have combed public archives looking for written and visual material to help represent the neighborhood can attest, the public record is sparse.[4] Now so prominent in our imaginations—nearly mythical—the value of the neighborhood's ecology, history, and cultures are finally being recognized.

In the beginning, the neighborhood we now call the Lower Ninth Ward developed downriver from the French Quarter as a plantation economy gave way to the growth of the city. In the mid to late 1800s, large tracts of land were carved up

Left: Cypress swamps in the Lower Ninth Ward. courtesy of the Percy Viosca, Jr. Collection, LSU Libraries Special Collections. *Right:* The Doullut Steamboat House No. 2 at 503 Egania Street in the Holy Cross neighborhood. Retired steamboat pilot Milton Doullut built two identical houses in 1905 and 1913. They have come to represent the neighborhood's promiximity to water, as well as many Ninth Ward residents' occupational connections to the river.[8] Photograph by Rachel Breunlin.

into smaller lots and turned into a new neighborhood. During the first half of the 20th century, Italian, Irish, and German immigrants and African Americans lived in and around the Holy Cross neighborhood, located on the natural levee of the Mississippi River.[5] The city hadn't developed a comprehensive drainage system, and this natural levee—a sliver of land physically attached to the curved path of the river—was the only suitable place for settlement. Beyond the higher ground were cypress swamps and salt marsh.[6]

In the 1920s, the Sewerage and Water Board built drainage canals in the lower–lying land between the natural levee and Bayou Bienvenue, which opened up this land for settlement.[7] Many African Americans took advantage of this marginal but inexpensive land, and bought property. At a time of *de jure* segregation, they turned to their own organizations for social and economic support. Black churches featured prominently. One of the legendary figures of the Spiritualist Church in New Orleans, for instance, developed her

Top: Photograph of the Lower Ninth Ward by New Orleans Sewerage and Water Board, courtesy of the New Orleans City Archives. *Bottom:* Photograph of Mother Catherine Seals, an influential figure in the Spiritual Church in New Orleans, donated to the museum by Wayne Hill. The picture is from his mother, Mary Hill Andrews, who is a licensed minister and a follower of Mother Catherine's Christian/Spiritual movement. He explains, "Mother Catherine was a religious leader and a community activist in the Lower Ninth Ward." The *Louisiana Weekly* wrote in her obituary, "Her followers and admirers are counted in the thousands. White, black, the learned and the illiterate, the rich and the poor vied to do her honor." [11] Spiritual churches around New Orleans continue to exist. The most well known, the Israelite Divine Spiritual Church on Frenchmen Street, is where members of the Hill family still worship.

following in the neighborhod. Mother Catherine Seals was an artist, a missionary, and a well–respected spiritual leader at a time when women had just won the right to vote. In 1922, she bought property on Charbonnet Street and, over the rest of the decade, turned the land into a "religious village" that extended more than a city block. [9]

In the 1950s, Elizabeth Cousins Rogers and her husband, Walter Rogers, moved into the neighborhood from the French Quarter. The two were long–term white residents; Walter was an organizer for the International Workers of the World (IWW) and Elizabeth was a writer who had worked alongside Dorothy Parker at *Vogue* magazine. Civil rights activists, they paid attention to the relationships between their black and white neighbors. Elizabeth writes:

> A block from our house live Corrie and Ida Mae Dixon, our two best friends and neighbors…They were raised on a Mississippi farm owned by their parents. Corrie and Ida Mae often entertain us with reminiscences of cows, mules, greedy acquaintances and neighboring white folks, some of whom surprisingly still lend a friendly hand with reclaiming stolen cows or settling intricate legal matters. Both married, they had to divorce uncooperative husbands. For some 30 years, working in hotels and white folks' families…they've managed, by heaven knows what self-denial, to clear the mortgage on two small house-and-lots, side by side on Tupelo Street. [10]

Although the land was mostly owned by the people who lived there, residents still had to contend with larger city and state plans for their neighborhood. Between the heyday of Mother Catherine Seals and the the arrival of the Rogers, the neighborhood's geography dramatically changed when the Port Authority decided to build a shipping canal on land it had purchased from the Ursuline nuns near Poland Avenue. Built between 1918–1923, the Inner Harbor Navigation Canal, known to New Orleanians simply as the Industrial Canal, runs from the Mississippi River to Lake Pontchartrain. In the decades that followed, it was connected to the Gulf of Mexico through two other man-made canals—the Mississippi River Gulf Outlet (MRGO) and the Intercoastal Waterway.[12]

The Port Authority hoped that these large-scale landscape and hydrology modifications would increase business at the Port of New Orleans, but they had significant impacts on the lives of residents. The deep draft canal split the Ninth Ward into "Upper" (upriver) and "Lower" (downriver) sections that were connected by the St. Claude Bridge. Javon Booker, a high school student in 2003, reflects on his relationship to it:

> I've been [in the Lower Ninth Ward] all my life, crossing the big, old, and grey St. Claude Bridge over the Industrial Canal to go to school and other parts of the city. "Uncle Claude" isn't one of the fanciest bridges in the world, but one which I've grown used to. In the morning I like to watch the sun bounce reflectively across the dark unsee-throughable water, calm and peaceful except for the little fish jumping up and down and birds coveting bits and pieces as if it's their own luxury item.[13]

In the event of hurricanes, however, the peaceful repose Javon writes about is disrupted by threats

Industrial Canal from the Lower Ninth Ward's levee, by Percy Viosca, Jr. Photograph courtesy of the Percy Viosca, Jr. Photograph Collection, Mss. 4948, Louisiana and Lower Mississippi Valley Collections, LSU Libraries, Baton Rouge, LA.

of storm surges from the Gulf of Mexico that can push their way into up the canals and overcome insufficient levee systems.[14]

The dangers caused by the close proximity to waterways weren't the first to threaten the area. Since April of 1927, when the Mississippi River Commission, led by the white elite in New Orleans, decided to dynamite part of the Mississippi River levee in St. Bernard Parish to save New Orleans from the flooding, residents of the Lower Ninth Ward have felt that their part of the city was physically and politically at risk from more powerful forces.[15] When storm surges traveling up the shipping canals overtopped the levees in the Lower Nine during Hurricane Betsy in 1965, and again with Katrina in 2005, many residents felt they were subjected to a government conspiracy that sacrificed their land for more affluent areas of the city.[16]

In 1957, the Judge Seeber Bridge, connecting the Upper and Lower sides of the Ninth Ward, was built at North Claiborne Avenue. Known to city residents at the "Claiborne Avenue bridge," it became a safe haven when Hurricane Betsy's storm surge overwhelmed the Industrial Canal's levee system in the Lower Nine. Photograph of Betsy evacuees on September 12, 1965 by G.E. Arnold, courtesy of *The Times-Picayune*.

For African American residents, there is another layer of structural obstacles around racial discrimination. Throughout the first half of the 20th century, the Lower Ninth Ward was a mixed neighborhood whose institutions were segregated. Neighbors may have helped each other, kids played together on the streets, but schools, churches, and businesses remained separate. In the 1950s, Black residents in the Lower Ninth Ward were actively organizing for their rights to vote and brought lawsuits against Orleans Parish to desegregate the public schools. According to historian Juliette Landphair,

> Local attorneys later recalled that few black New Orleanians dared to risk their families' well being and livelihoods in such a public way. Fueled by the hope of civil rights and better neighborhoods, however, some Lower Ninth Ward residents believed it was a risk worth taking.[17]

School desegregation for the entire district began in the neighborhood in 1960. According to education activist Aesha Rasheed, "In that year, the School Board subjected black students who applied to attend a white school to an admissions test and finally allowed a carefully

selected group of black girls (boys were deemed too threatening) to attend William Frantz [in the Upper Ninth Ward] and McDonogh No. 19 [in the Lower Nine]."[18] The actual integration brought international attention to the community when white mothers pulled their children out of the schools and then began congregating outside the elementary school buildings, shouting racial slurs at the young girls.[19]

Many white families who did not participate in these racial attacks were impacted by the polarizing climate. Some resented that their working class neighborhood was the first one chosen by the city while more affluent parts of town remained unchanged. Others said they didn't feel safe around other white neighbors' violence or the anger their Black neighbors felt as they were forced to defend themselves. In the years that followed, many moved across the Parish line to St. Bernard. Others stayed, only to leave after the city was slow to help the neighborhood rebuild after Hurricane Betsy. Looking at the photographs of the evacuation of the Lower Ninth Ward in 1965 and again in 2005 provides a glimpse into this major shift in population. From 1940 to 1970, the "nonwhite" population of the Lower Ninth Ward increased from 31 to 73 percent. By 2000, the neighborhood was 90 percent African American.[20]

African American journalist Will Sutton grew up in the Lower Ninth Ward in the 1960s playing kickball and catching crawfish in the canals, listening to the Holy Cross band practice after

The Battle Ground Baptist Church, located on Flood Street in the Lower Ninth Ward. The migration between the parishes did not happen in just one direction. The African American community of Fazendeville, located on the site of the Battle of New Orleans in St. Bernard Parish, was demolished in 1964 to make way for a national historical park. Over 45 families were forced to move, and many relocated to the Lower Ninth Ward, where they rebuilt the Battle Ground.[23] Photographs by Rachel Breunlin.

school, and using paper Japanese lanterns to illuminate nights in a neighborhood that still felt rural. But as a reporter, he looked back at how his neighborhood was represented and found it disconcerting:

> Other city neighborhoods seemed to make the news for all kinds of reasons. Bad news. Good news. Breaking news. Feature news. When it came to our old neighborhood, however, it seemed that we only made television or made the paper when someone was shot and killed or when there was enough water to show cars slowly driving through the floodwaters.[21]

Perhaps this is why residents of the neighborhood are so proud of Antoine "Fats" Domino, who still lived in the neighborhood after becoming an the international R&B legend. The story is told over and over again to demonstrate how there was something special both about this place and about the man who didn't leave even when he had enough fame and fortune to travel the world. A friend of Fats, Haydee Ellis, said:

> The Ninth Ward was a real community…People walked to his house to visit all the time. He was so relaxed with his friends and the musicians he knows. Strangers could knock on the door, and if Fats was up to it, he'd share whatever he was cooking, and he'd play the piano for them. He'd shake hands with people on a tour bus.[22]

Like many of his neighbors, Fats was rescued from the top of his roof during Hurricane Katrina. Afterward, the tour buses driving through the neighborhood changed. The devastating

Street scene of the Lower Ninth Ward from records of the Sewerage and Water Board, courtesy of the New Orleans City Archives.

flooding caused by the breach of the Industrial Canal made headlines for weeks and created a media circus. As the city was drained, large parts of the Lower Ninth Ward remained closed to residents. To make matters worse, while they were displaced, worried about missing relatives and friends, and unsure whether their houses were still standing, residents heard early policy reports that the "low-lying areas" like parts of the Lower Nine shouldn't be rebuilt. The stark contrast between top-down urban planning and the grief of an exiled community caused a huge outcry from residents and others committed to social justice and the right to return to the city.[24] On December 15, 2005, the City Council of New Orleans passed a resolution that all areas of the city "should get equal treatment and should be rebuilt simultaneously."[25]

In the Lower Ninth Ward, residents, scholars, and activists began organizing against the profiling of the neighborhood, which had entered the national consciousness as another poverty-stricken urban area. The emerging counternarrative was based on a simple fact: 54% of households in Lower Ninth Ward were owner-occupied.[26] The majority of the land didn't belong to people outside the community—the property, and consequently the decisions about rebuilding, would mostly be controlled by the people who lived there.

But owning land in the Lower Nine was just the beginning. 3,500 units of housing were flooded in the neighborhood, and 1,000 had to be demolished due to extreme structural damage.[27] Recognizing the massive devastation and slow rebuilding progress, large numbers of people from around the country began volunteering their time, money, and energy to help the neighborhood recover. As they connected with residents of the Lower Ninth Ward who were beginning to gut their homes and think about rebuilding,

Photographers Keith Calhoun and Chandra McCormick, who grew up in the Lower Ninth Ward, found inspiration in Fats Domino's commitment to the neighborhood. Keith told a *New York Times* reporter, "Me, Fat and them, we always kept returning to the hood. Me and Chandra, we could have gone somewhere else and competed...but my work is for the people."[28] Their Holy Cross studio, and a significant amount of their work, was destroyed during Katrina. In the wake of the storm, Chandra created an informal installation outside their home with salvaged negatives, prints, and photo equipment, including a matted photograph [*top*] by Keith Calhoun. They have since gone on to start the L9 Center for the Arts in their neighborhood. Photographs by Rachel Breunlin.

they got to know the history of the neighborhood. Many, it seems, left feeling that they had been transformed by the experience. On the levee wall near the Claiborne Avenue Bridge is a stenciled sign that says, "New Orleans gave me paciencia y passion [patience and passion]."

The House of Dance & Feathers was one of the many places in the neighborhood to receive help, first as a construction site, and then as a semi–public museum. As people have come to his neighborhood, the museum has served as a kind of orientation center where Ronald explains the culture of the neighborhood to visitors and advocates for their support in the rebuild. He's also connected volunteers to other neighbors who were working on their own reconstruction. Since 2005, he has worked with university groups, scholars, journalists, tourists, and artists to help them locate the Lower Ninth Ward in the larger histories of New Orleans, southern Louisiana, and the diaspora cultures of the Black Atlantic.

The coalition that formed around the rebuilding of the museum and house on Tupelo Street is impressive, but can also be seen as part of a massive grassroots movement. The writer Rebecca Solnit, who visited New Orleans a number of times in the year after the storm, wrote about the incredible influx of labor, material, and money that has arrived around the city without governmental support:

> The list of who came to help sounds like the setup for a joke: A Black Panther, an accountant, a bunch of Methodists and the mayor of Portland walk into a bar. Or if you prefer, Brad Pitt, some graduate students, lots of young anarchists, and the Sierra Club walk in. No one yet has assessed the scale of the volunteer influx

Robert Green was one of the first residents to move back to the area of the Lower Ninth Ward closest to the levee breach. He lost both his mother and his granddaughter in the flood. Next to his FEMA trailer is a handwritten sign to all the visitors who pass by: "We want our country to love us as much as we love our country. The strength of our country belongs to us all. Mr Bush: Rebuild New Orleans, The Lower Ninth Ward, Cross the Canal, Tennessee Street, NOT IRAQ. Tourist: Tell Your Senator, Your Representative, Our President." His message emphasizing equal rights as American citizens recalls a critique of early media reports referring to New Orleans residents as "refugees." Photograph by Rachel Breunlin.

to New Orleans, which has been compared to the Freedom Summer during the civil rights era but has far out–stripped it in sheer numbers. It's a safe underestimate to say that more than 100,000 volunteers have come from out of town.[29]

Many organizations have developed with the help of coalitions of people from within and outside the Lower Ninth Ward. To name just a few, Common Ground Collective, Global Green, and Brad Pitt's Make it Right Foundation have been working at various scales—gutting houses, developing infrastructure around energy conservation, and building new homes in the most devastated parts of the neighborhood. Others, such as Neighborhood Empowerment Network Association and the Holy Cross Neighborhood Association, are organized and run by residents of the Lower Nine. Ronald, recognized in his role as community leader by many of these organizations, has been a supporter of other projects, giving speeches at the Association of Community Organization for Reform Now (ACORN) events after the storm, serving on the board of the Lower Ninth Ward Village, bringing a portable version of the House of Dance & Feathers to the Sankofa Market, and holding events at the museum.[30]

In the months leading up to the November 2007 performances of *Waiting for Godot* in the Lower Ninth Ward and Gentilly, Ronald and the creative director, Paul Chan, hosted a dinner party for the community partners and cast at the House of Dance & Feathers. A few weeks later, at the opening night of the play, the Big Nine Social and Pleasure Club led an audience of over 600 through the back-a-town streets of the Lower Nine. On bulldozed lots, where Samuel Becket's set design instructions, "A Country Road, A Tree, Evening," were eerily easy to recreate, people from around the country and city sat together on bleachers to watch the play.[31]

On nights like this, the Lower Nine becomes a cosmopolitan place. The danger, of course, is that for newcomers, the neighborhood will only be seen as a backdrop—another kind of media created by outsiders that projects its vision of disaster and/or race onto a place with its own specificities. The strength of the *Waiting for Godot* project was that Paul built the production around a network of local and national collaborators. At the dinners, courses, meetings, and rehearsels leading up to the performances, spaces were created for multiple narratives to develop through dialogue. In its own way, the production supported the grassroots organizing efforts that continue to break down monolithic representations of the Lower Ninth Ward and New Orleans.

Left: Willard "Shorty" Walker, Charlotte "Minnie" Lewis, and Robert "Big Bob" Starks of the Big Nine Social & Pleasure Club bring in the audience gathered to see *Waiting for Godot. Right:* J. Kyle Manzay and Wendell Pierce, under the direction of the Classical Theatre of Harlem, perform in the Lower Ninth Ward. Photographs courtesy of Paul Chan.

While the production of *Waiting for Godot* brought in people from all over the city to the Lower Ninth Ward, the crowning of Ronald as the "king of the French Quarters" recognized his work in the neighborhood as a cultural translator, and brought the masking traditions of Mardi Gras Indians into the predominantly white, bohemian countercultures of the Faubourg Marigny and French Quarter. Members of the Krewe du Jieux marched as his royal honor guard and passed out flyers that made connections between the 2008 parade theme, "The Magical Misery Tour," which invites satirical critiques of the state of recovery in New Orleans, and the political struggles of cultural groups Ronald's museum often exhibits. Photographs by Devin Meyers of Fotos for Humanity.

J.A.I.L.
THE JIEUXISH AFRIKAN INJUN LEAGUE
Hand Delivered OFFICIAL PROPAGANDA –
WARRANT of Arrest Benefits
In Honor of Ronald W. Lewis,
King of Krewe du Vieux's Magical Misery Tour,
The Jieuxish Afrikan Injun League has cornered the market on TSURIS

MISERY!
YOU WANT TSURIS? WE GOT TSURIS!

Are your people under perpetual threat of genocide?
Does the smell of bacon sometimes reduce you to tears?
Have you called your mother?
Still waiting for reparations for slavery and segregation?
Is your road home full of potholes?
Have you been sold down the River Babylon?
Did you used to wander freely with your tribe?
Do you have reservations about your reservation?
What? You can't even get a reservation on your reservation?

Prisons are America's largest and most patriotic growth industry and the members of J.A.I.L. propose building the world's largest SuperPrison right here in New Orleans... where all the public housing used to stand.
JOIN the Jieuxish Afrikan Injun League and

GO TO J.A.I.L. FREE!
FREE room and board, 3 squares a day; utilities paid!
FREE Health Care – Rx over the counter and under!
FREE Education – G.E.D., J.D. or JAILhouse pharmacy!
FREE Unsupervised Exercise Programs and Weight Training
Would you like to explore your sexuality? Enjoy the companionship
of a roomate, or go for the solitary experience!

steady meaningful work, think of it as a kibbutz!
TSURIS WITH A SMILE

Other events in the Lower Ninth Ward have followed with varying degrees of input and participation from residents. In November of 2008, Prospect.1, the largest biennial of international contemporary art ever organized in the United States, opened in New Orleans with a heavy emphasis on site-specific pieces in the neighborhood. Visitors drive slowly through the backstreets with open maps, looking for art amongst the ruins and islands of rebuilding. Ronald's museum is listed as a "cultural site." [32]

Coming into the House of Dance & Feathers, visitors will enter another cosmopolitan space— one that is based on Ronald's personal story of growing up in the Lower Ninth Ward, but continues to grow as he discovers and incorporates other traditions from around the city, country, and globe into his museum. The Katrina narrative, and the wide network of people who helped rebuild the museum, are also on display, but this era is only part of the story. The space urges you to connect the storm to the rest of the neighborhood's history. A work in progress, it celebrates the possibilities that are still being created. It is a place where any visitor can get involved, whether from around the corner or across the world.

Ronald W. Lewis works on a beaded patch for a Mardi Gras Indian costume at his demonstration booth
at the New Orleans Jazz & Heritage Festival's Louisiana Folklife Village.

The Multifaceted Life of Ronald W. Lewis

The quarters on a plantation in Lafourche Parish. Photograph by Ronald W. Lewis, fall 2005.

My mom's family moved to New Orleans for a better way of life.

She said life wasn't good for her as a girl growing up on a plantation in Lafourche Parish. Behind that bayou is a lifetime of misery for all those workers in the sugar cane fields. It was brutal the way people were treated. Those are the exact words to use. She talked about the hangings at Lafourche Crossing along Highway One and how, once, a man was sick and couldn't go to work. They went to the quarters and shot him.

Growing up, she used to tell me, "When I die, do not bring me back to that place," but she didn't have a problem going to visit. Her brother, Clarence, still lived on Abby Plantation. We'd go past the big house into the quarters where he lived by the train tracks. In the summer, I remember walking at night from Abby Plantation to Coulon Plantation with candles.

From what my mom explains, her parents came over from another place called White Plantation. I'll tell you a strange thing. My family name was White, just like White Plantation, but when they moved off that plantation, they changed their name from White to Wright. They changed their names to have some distance from these people that they came from. A lot of people made adjustments when they left off the plantations cause that was their way of freedom.

In the 1940s, my parents bought some land in the Lower Ninth Ward at 1911 Deslonde Street and built our family home. I was born in 1951. Our neighborhood wasn't a subdivision like Pontchartrain Park near the lake, but Black people were able to buy properties down here and build their houses at a time when housing discrimination denied people the right to move into certain areas. The men, and their children, would carry wood all day, stacking it in their yard to build their homes. Whenever somebody got money together to pour a sidewalk, the men in the neighborhood would come together and pour them. Those people brought with them country values, and I clearly understood in later years what the teaching of the old people was: They didn't have nothing, but they had each other. They drove that into their children.

Mama raised six of us. Her husband, Mr. Irving Dickerson—we called him DaDa or Uncle Plum, he had many titles for one man—worked at the sugar refinery and she did days' work, ironing clothes and cleaning a house on Tennessee Street for this white lady, Ducky Meyer. In the early 1960s, DaDa died after a long sickness. No one had to be asked to contribute to the household. It was just automatic. I sold cold drink bottles, ran errands to the stores, and cut grass—whatever it took, I tried to be a part of keeping the household moving.

I never could remember my oldest brother, Walter, living at home because he was a seaman at an early age. He would bring big kites and china sets with fancy little teacups back from overseas. As a boy, I used to just stand there look at my mama's china cabinet with all these unique things you couldn't touch. When she passed, my sister Stella asked me, "Well, what do you want out of the house?" I told her the blue plates with the city of San Francisco on them, and a set of figurines with a stamp on the bottom that said "Made in Occupied Japan." They were my great inheritance.

Porcelain figurines Ronald inherited from his mother, Rebecca Wright Dickerson. Photograph by Devin Meyers of Fotos for Humanity.

Photograph of a banana wharf in New Orleans, courtesy of the Frank B. Moore Collection, Earl K. Long Library, University of New Orleans.

We were a rich culture being a working class community.

Most of our fathers and kinfolk were hardworking men. They were primarily longshoremen, and they worked the Mississippi River. They had industry along the Industrial Canal, too. Now the women didn't have great jobs—a lot of the women were like my mother doing housework, pressing clothes—but many of the men were part of the Longshoremen's Union.

You had a blend of Louisiana and Mississippi people in our neighborhood. This fella Anzo and a blues player named Boogie Bill Webb lived in the neighborhood. On Saturday mornings, they would come out there on Anzo's porch and crank up them old guitars. They would drink their corn liquor and play their blues until dusk dark. You looked forward to that every Saturday morning, and it carried the rural feel of the Lower Ninth Ward.

Food in our neighborhood came from the different places women grew up. My friend Peter Alexander's family was a traditional, New Orleans Creole family, and Ms. Geraldine and them's cooking wasn't the same as my mama's even though they lived right across the street from each other. She would do homemade pork chops, creamed potatoes, and gumbo.

My mother was from the country where she made biscuits and cornbread mush. Peter and I would go out and pick blackberries off the levees and my mama would make blackberry dumplings. Our next-door neighbor, Ms. Skipper, made some of the greatest crawfish bits in the world, and Ms.Mars made some of the greatest chocolate cake in the world.

People had chicken and ducks, and a couple of people had pigs. We always did have green space through the drainage canals. In those canals, we crawfished, crabbed, and fished. And once we crossed Florida Avenue, the marshland around Bayou Bienvenue was right there.

The only time we used to get to watch TV all night was when there was talk of a hurricane coming.

Betsy came at night in September of 1965. I was going to school then at Alfred Lawless Junior High School. My brother Larry, who was just a few years older than me, came inside and told us water was in the streets. We turned off the TV, grabbed our little bags, and by the time we got outside, the water was waist high. We went across the street to where Peter Alexander and them lived in a two-story building. That's where a lot of people evacuated to.

Larry and some of the older fellas in the neighborhood rescued a lot of people. They were taking doors off of houses and using them as rafts to bring people to higher ground. When the sun rose the next morning, you really saw reality.

The water was up to the roof of the house, and our ducks were just swimming around in a circle, right around the house. I remember that like it was yesterday.

Larry stepped up to the plate. He started to work on the cleanup trucks. He got an apartment right off of Poland Avenue and moved us out of the naval base, where we were staying after our house flooded. We stayed in an apartment, and worked on our house on Deslonde Street. They didn't have FEMA then. I remember Red Cross gave us a voucher for furniture, and they gave people vouchers for materials to help them rebuild. There wasn't no contractors doing the work. It was the people—these young men, under the leadership of the grown men like Mr. Skipper and Mr. Buckner, who took care of their families and rebuilt our houses.

As rooms got finished, we moved back home. During that time, they had tin garbage cans, and Mama would take wood and charcoal and grill out of it. That's how we would heat our water to bathe at night and everything.

I always did have a passion for education.

I went to George Washington Carver for high school. It was built in the late 1950s, and served three communities—the Desire Public Housing Development area, the Seabrook area near the lakefront, and the Lower Ninth Ward. By serving all those areas, you had a chance to end up having great friendships from people from other areas of the Ninth Ward and Pontchartrain Park.

I was growing up in the time of transition, from the time when our parents and grandparents were being beaten and bit by dogs fighting for their civil rights to the Black Panthers and them saying, "Say it loud, I'm Black and I'm proud."

You know, the clenched fist and the holding the shotgun up in the air saying, "If you hit me, I'm gonna hit you back."

I was a sympathizer. I wore dashikis and black berets on my head, bootlace bracelets from fellas who had been to Vietnam. I sold Black Panther Party newspapers on Canal Street and knew some of the Black Panthers who worked out of the Desire Project personally. They used to have the Nation of Islam down here in the Lower Ninth Ward and I used to go to the mosque and got some of the teaching of Elijah Mohammad as well as the Pan-African thinking of Black Crusaders Incorporated. I was just out there soaking up education that is still part of my self-identity today.

My plan after graduation was to be a longshoreman because that was the big-money job in my community. All my cousins and everybody else in the neighborhood worked on the riverfront. But when I finished school, I worked a couple years at the Ear, Eye, Nose, and Throat Hospital at Tulane and Elks before working for New Orleans Public Service. My brother-in-law, Leonard Keesley, who's married to my sister Stella, got me a job there in 1971.

At first I was a custodian, but then I wanted more money, so I trained to work out there on the streetcar tracks. It was a different world. The foreman was a throwback type where a Black man couldn't say nothing to him. Most of the fellas I worked with came out of those plantation regions—the Mississippi Delta or from around St. Francisville and Angola. They knew how to relate to that type of life, but I didn't. I grew up down here in the Lower Ninth Ward, which is known for being fearless and organized. I could never fix my mouth to call the foreman Mr. Freddie. I just called him Freddie. My name was always Ronald, you know? Some of them told me, "Man, them people gonna fire you."

Here I am, young, wild and crazy. Union organizers started coming to me and asking me to sign up people to get a union card.

The first organizing I did was with Amalgamated Transit Union. They'd just organized the bus drivers, and were trying to organize the track workers—the maintenance. But at the time, the racial divide was bigger in the maintenance department because the majority of the mechanics were white. They were living large and didn't want a union. I went to talking to people. Some people ran from me; some people came to me. When it was all said and done, we lost that election.

Around 1975, the International Brotherhood of Electrical Workers (IBEW) came to me. They organized the power department of New Orleans Public Service with the line workers and plant workers. Their next move was maintenance. I took some more cards, we fought the good battle, and we won. In 1977, we became Local 1700-4 of the IBEW.

Being a union organizing rep taught me a lot about public speaking. I learned how to document and put things in the right place because you were dealing with people's livelihoods. If you had on the job problems and you went in to management and weren't prepared, they would eat you up and spit you out. In my early years, that's what they did to me. I was very aggressive. Every time I walked in that office, they were prepared for me. They would beat me up with words and I would come out feeling dumb. I started watching more documentaries and reading more. Over the years, I got better at it, and management started having respect for my skills—of being able to communicate with them.

My wife, Charlotte "Minnie" Hill, is part of the Hill-Lastie-Andrews family. Music has been the foundation of their family for as long as I've been involved.

We met in 1970 when she was still a student at Carver Senior High. I think she's one of 16 children, and I'm gonna say 13 of that 16 made their homes down here in the Lower Ninth Ward—round the corner, in the same block, and everything. Her grandparents' house is right down the street on Tupelo.

I grew up in a home environment, and we never did rent. Going into them early years of our marriage, I wanted a similar life to the one we had at 1911 Deslonde—the yard, the privacy. I told Minnie, "Well, we both working. If you find a house down there in the Lower Ninth, we'll buy it." Fortunately, she was working at Charity Hospital and a nurse named Ms. Evans' sister wanted to sell her house. This is how we ended up on Tupelo Street.

When we moved in April of 1978, they were just closing in the drainage canals, and all the streets were dug up. Our son Rashad was born in May. He's seven years younger than his older brother, Ronaldo.

An exhibit of Lower Ninth Ward musicians on display at the museum traces family and neighborhood connections. Photograph by Rachel Breunlin. *Top left:* A signed publicity photograph donated by Joseph "Fish Daddy" Lastie Jr., drummer for the Preservation Hall Jazz Band. *Top center:* A publicity photograph of Antoine Dominique "Fats" Domino. Photograph donated by one of his road managers, Coot Parker. *Top right:* A photograph of Herlin Riley, Jr., drummer for Wynton Marsalis at the Lincoln Center and grandson of Frank Lastie, a drummer in the Spiritualist Church in the Lower Ninth Ward. Photograph by Ronald W. Lewis. *Bottom right:* A page of *Offbeat* magazine featuring Jesse "Ooh Poo Pah Doo" Hill, whose grandchildren include James, Troy (aka Trombone Shorty), and Darnell Andrews. *Bottom center:* The Lastie family. Photograph donated by Joe Lastie, Jr. *Bottom left:* A publicity photograph of Oliver "Who Shot the La La" Morgan.

Top: Minnie with Rashad and Ronaldo, standing on the neutral ground on Tupelo Street. *Bottom:* A backyard full of boys at the Lewises' house on Tupelo Street. Photographs by Ronald W. Lewis.

A sign Ronald's neighbor, Beulah Coley Smith, kept in her house before the storm is now on display in the museum.
Photograph by Devin Meyers of Fotos for Humanity.

With my two sons, my backyard stayed full of boys. Minnie cooked and fed them all. Our neighbor, Ms. Beulah Coley Smith, was the mama of our neighborhood. She fed everybody, too. She grew up in Boutte, Louisiana, and would draw on those country traditions. She would fry catfish, shuck peas, and made the best fried bread. It's similar to the kind Houma Indians make and must be a regional food because my mama used to make it, too. We called our youngest son Fat. Beulah would call him, "Fatman, you come over here and get this food." She helped us raise our family when Minnie and I were both working,

In my spare time, I was helping to make Mardi Gras Indian costumes. Ronaldo didn't pick up my love for it. His passion is cars. Fat went to school in the Sixth Ward and was in the Bell Middle School marching band. He had his fair share of culture shock leaving his community to go to school, but he also learned a lot about music and masked a few years with our tribe, the

Lois Andrews, a member of the Money Wasters Social & Pleasure Club and daughter of Lower Ninth Ward musician Jesse Hill, dances on top of her son's casket as his jazz funeral goes down Orleans Avenue next to the Lafitte Public Housing Development. Darnell "D-Boy" Andrews was shot in the Lafitte in May of 1995. D-Boy's brothers, James and Troy "Trombone Shorty" Andrews, are also musicians and were part of the band that played during his second line. In 1997, James went on to record an album with the New Birth Brass Band that included the title track "D-Boy." Photograph by Eric Waters.

Choctaw Hunters. I had the joy of watching my kids grow up and have their own children, but I was also seeing so many of our young people die on the streets of New Orleans. It got to the point where I got tired of going to funerals. I got tired of crying.

Growing up in the 1960s and 70s, they had so much training to offer young people. When these Republicans came into office, they shut down all the social programs. Then they said they wanted to control crime, but didn't offer other opportunities. We had to develop ones in our own communities to try to counteract the violence. We did it through music, Mardi Gras Indian gangs and second lines, our churches, and schools. I've worked to get kids enrolled in job training programs. But even with all these efforts, we still end up memorializing some of our young ones on the t-shirts we wear to their funerals.

The new millenium brought in a change in me. I retired from the Regional Transit Authority in 2002, and started to think about the rest of my life. I started there when I was 20, and I retired at 50. From that point on, I said, "The rest of my life is gonna be for me." I walked out the doors and never looked back. I started building a new life and concentrating on the House of Dance & Feathers.

Glen David Andrews, cousin of Darnell "D-Boy" Andrews, plays the trombone during a street parade in New Orleans. He says his family traces their roots back to "free people of color who migrated from Violet to the Ninth Ward. A lot of people of the Ninth Ward went to the Sixth Ward, where I grew up with James, D-Boy, and Trombone Shorty—they were my playmates.

"The Hills kind of helped me become the musician I am. I needed those people to break those barriers. I met Jesse Hill at his coffin. The day we played his funeral is the day I actually knew who he was. For me, to wake up in the morning knowing I have to play a funeral is a beautiful thing. People are gonna be sad and cry tears, but when all's said and done, it's gonna be a celebration."

Also known as a vocalist, Glen David wrote the lyrics to "Knock with Me-Rock with Me," a popular second line song covered by the Lil Rascals, the New Birth Brass Band, and others. In the song, he asks, "Who that shot D-Boy, y'all?" [33] Considering the deaths of so many young men, he says, "Look what you have in New Orleans—extreme poverty. What comes with poverty? Drugs and violence. If you don't have education or anyone teaching you, then it becomes generations." He sees his commitment to music and parades as a positive contribution to the streets of New Orleans, "Anything you put negative with music puts me to tears. People come to second lines to socialize and get along with each other. When I see people dance, that's the 'thank you.' Yesterday, a kid said, 'I want to play a horn just like you.' That's the ultimate." Photograph by Andy Levin.

A coconut made for the Zulu Social Aid and Pleasure Club's Mardi Gras day parade takes on a new twist after Hurricane Katrina. One part of Arthur and Gina Vigne's three part series "The Three Wise Monkeys," made at the Louisiana Folklife Village at the New Orleans Jazz & Heritage Festival and now on display at the museum, this "Speak No Evil" coconut calls out the names of places hit hard in New Orleans: "9th Ward, Lakeview, N.O. East," as well as other states along the Gulf Coast. Photograph by Devin Meyers of Fotos for Humanity.

The Katrina Story

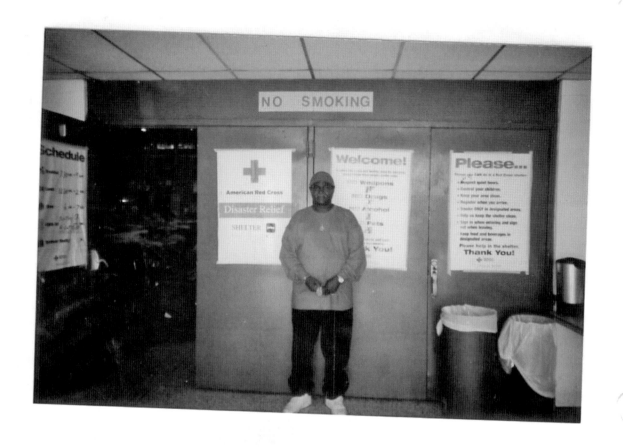

Ronald W. Lewis
Betsy - 65
Katrina - 05
Survivor

When I left New Orleans that Tuesday morning after Katrina, the only thing I knew was that I was heading in the direction of Thibodaux, Louisiana.

Minnie and I rode out the hurricane in a hotel, but by the time the chaos was over, we were in the same boat as the people in the Convention Center and the Superdome—trying to find a place to be safe. My wife went to Atlanta with Rashad and my other son, Ronaldo, was in Florida. I talked to them and said, "I'm holding it down. I'm going to be okay." Here is someone that spent their life in an urban city and ends up in a place where sugar cane is still king.

I have a tattoo on my arm I had done while I was in Thibodaux. I wanted something to say, "Twice in my life, this happened." Hurricane Betsy in 1965 and Hurricane Katrina in 2005. I call them the two black holes in my life. After Betsy, the fishermen of St. Bernard Parish were telling the government that the MRGO canal was gonna come back to haunt them. Over the years, they went to telling about the loss of wetlands, and it fell on a deaf ear. In the end, it came to the light. The people of St. Bernard said, "We told y'all that this thing was gonna destroy the city, not just the Parish."

In Thibodaux, I spent a lot of time at Camp Stopher, a shelter set up at Nicholls State University. There were people in that shelter from the Ninth Ward—the Desire Projects, the Lower Nine, even someone from Tupelo Street. They just ended up on the same bus during the evacuation of New Orleans. Some people went back to the city to see the damage, and brought back reports and pictures. One woman showed me a picture of a tanker sitting behind her house in the Lower Ninth Ward. She said, "It floated off the railroad, that's how it did me. There's oil up in the house. Fungus. Katrina just tore my little house up. I'm glad I wasn't in there."

One of my club members, Ricky Gettridge, had a cot next to mine. At night, we played the tambourine and sang Mardi Gras Indian songs. It sounded like home.

Opposite page: The first page of Ronald's photo documentary project on his evacuation and exile in Thibodaux, Louisiana. *Above:* The shelter at Stopher Gym at Nicholls State University in Thibodaux, Louisiana. *Right:* The schedule of meal times and "lights out." Photographs by Ronald W. Lewis.

The Lewis home [*in front*] and the original House of Dance & Feathers [*small white building in back*] after Katrina. Dan Etheridge, who acted as one of the team coordinators in the rebuilding, reflects on the give and take that went into the project, "So many big ideas came out of the *ReInhabiting NOLA* conference, and while we compiled these carefully and submitted them to all the proper planning processes, people with university, nonprofit, or community resources knew that the pieces we could bite off and actually build had to be a manageable scale. Ronald's house and museum was such a great project for us to get our heads around because while it was just one house among many, it represented so much more. I wish I could I say that I actually built the museum, but my role was more of a team coordinator.

"If you survey the popular press, it would seem that all that has happened was that we helped Ronald and his family; in actuality it has been a great friendship where we have looked out for each other. Ronald has given me advice on marriage in the weeks leading up to my wedding, he has grilled his famous chicken wings for my family when they visited from Australia, and now he is giving me advice on fatherhood in advance of my first child. I count him as one of my closest friends." Photograph by Rachel Breunlin.

Partnerships and Alliances

It was early October 2005 when I met Steve Inskeep from National Public Radio. He was looking for a story about the Lower Ninth Ward and called Helen Regis, who's a cultural anthropologist, for recommendations. Helen's on the board of the House of Dance & Feathers and she passed my number on to him. I was still staying in Thibodaux with family. During that time, the only people coming to the Lower Ninth Ward were military and press people. All the regular people couldn't come into the community, although some snuck in. I came down here with Steve Inskeep, and that was really the beginning of my rebuilding process. I brought him into my old neighborhood and showed him where my family home once was on Deslonde Street and then came round to Tupelo Street and saw my home still standing. From that point on, I was on my way back. I said, "Well, I have a chance."

In November, I attended the *ReInhabiting NOLA* workshop in New Orleans that Helen and Dan invited me to. This workshop became the other phase of the rebuilding process. It was very interesting for me cause you had all these special people—city planners, urban architects, artists—you name it, they were there. They broke it up into groups, and here I am—this fella who worked on the streetcar tracks for 31 years—sitting with scholars from different universities. They were talking about the rebuilding process, and how they would like to do something in the Ninth Ward, which opened the door for me to tell them about my community. I told them about how I not only wanted to come back home, but wanted to help lead the way, to show how, through all this misery and despair, it could be done.

I shook hands with a lot of people and a lot of people responded. Dan said that the Tulane City Center, where he works, would become a partner to help rebuild the museum. My cousin Cliff Wright had already started clearing out my house. L.J. Goldstein, the 6t'9 Social & Pleasure Club, and other folks I met at *ReInhabiting NOLA* started helping, too. Dan asked a group of students from the University of Montana under these fellas Robin Saha and Tom Roy to clear out the museum. He also went to the Design/Build Summit in Arkansas that was called to organize the design community's response to Katrina. He promoted my museum as a rebuilding project and I got a call from an architect named Patrick Rhodes. He told me he ran a non-profit called Project Locus and taught at Kansas State University. He wanted to help rebuild the museum. Dan brought him down to visit me out

Top to bottom: Ronald's business cards on the mudcaked floor of the museum; the original museum after the storm; and a Big Nine fan destroyed by floodwaters. Photographs by Rachel Breunlin.

in Thibodaux and we took it from there. Out of that relationship, some very, very positive things grew. Our partnership created opportunities that neither one of us had before. And that odd couple relationship remains until today.

Ronald and Minnie looking at drawings of the house and museum at Project Locus' first design review in Spring 2006. Thinking back on the week leading up to the review, Jason Fedak recalls, "I remember like it was yesterday, the day we entered into the Lower Ninth Ward and feeling the shock of the destruction—the kind of devastation you see on the news, but still, devastation beyond anything I could have imagined. I remember thinking, 'There cannot be one person left down here.' We arrived at Ronald's house, and it was actually in much better shape than most in the neighborhood. A group of us worked hard day in and day out tearing out his house—Ronald popping in here and there for his usual motivational speech that kept us digging through the trash, rats, and the most God awful stuff that was left in the freezer during Katrina.

"Throughout the week, some people had stopped in and out to see the progress, but not many. Most of the traffic came from people wanting to see the devastation that Katrina left. On the last day, we finished up the cleaning process and began preparing for a barbeque. As optimistic as I wanted to be, I could not imagine more than a half dozen residents from the neighborhood showing up. But then the BBQ pit arrived on a trailer and was unloaded. Within a couple hours, the driveway, street, and yard were buzzing with people. For people from the Lower Ninth Ward, this was more than a BBQ, this was hope that their area would be rebuilt. The night was like a reunion; a sense of pride for their community. As it got dark, more than two dozen people surrounded us as we taped drawings on Ronald's house. We talked about our ideas while they stood around flashlights like we were putting on a show. When we got done I looked around and I can never forget that look on some of everyone's faces. In Ronald's exact words; 'This museum will serve as a beacon of light and will begin the rebuilding process.'" Photograph by Eric Wittman.

When Tom Roy found out there was an architect on board, he helped raise the money we needed to build through the Charles Engelhard Foundation. With the money in place, Patrick's students came down during their spring break to begin working on the project and we had one of our famous Tupelo barbeques. They pinned up a variety of designs on the back of my house. Minnie and I said, "We just wanna get back in our house. Y'all are architects. Y'all put it together." Down the line, I realized that architects really want the client, as they call us, to have input. As the project progressed, I got more involved as I understood they wanted to hear things from me.

Over the summer, Project Locus, with the help of students from Kansas State and other universities, rebuilt not only the museum, but our house. The students stayed at L.J.'s house in the Sixth Ward and drove down to the Lower Nine every

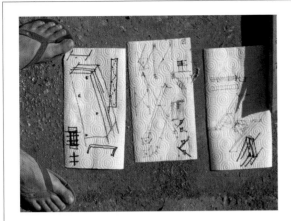

Top: Rebuilding Ronald's house and museum. *Bottom:* Eric Wittman, Aaron Schump, Ronald W. Lewis, Melody Jacobson, Brian Copeland, Patrick Rhodes, Noah Cahan, Ben Gauslin, and Tomas Martinek. Patrick recalls the routine that developed over the summer, "We spent our days working between the 384–square–foot museum and Ronald's house, eating BBQ from the rib man selling out of a beat up trailer on St. Claude Avenue, and turning towards the daiquiri shop in St. Bernard Parish as the sun went down. Natural leaders like Kyle Wedel and Tomas Martinek emerged, volunteers like Noah Cahan came for a week and ended up staying a month. Caitlin found companies to donate money and much needed materials. We had not only become a real team, but we were becoming a part of the community of Tupelo Street. Some of my fondest memories, and I'm sure for everyone else, were the nights we spent on the neutral ground down by Charles Napoleon's, or Yacky as he is known in the neighborhood, eating Demetrius Alexander's chicken, playing dominoes, drinking beer, and dispelling the myths long perpetuated that the Lower Ninth Ward was a dangerous, derelict place where white people only go to buy drugs. It had become our home, and we were proud of it." Photographs by Caitlin Heckathorn.

Over the summer, sunflowers were planted along the driveway of the Lewises' property while students from around the country came down to help rebuild the house and museum. Patrick Rhodes explains the process: "Initially, the plan for constructing the house and museum was to divide the team up into two groups, each dedicated to a specific structure. As the weeks progressed and the work continued, we soon understood that such compartmentalization was impossible and work between the two buildings occurred fluidly." Photographs by Caitlin Heckathorn.

day. They had a chance to understand about urban life, and that people who live in urban communities do have family values, do care about others, and do really want to have a better life. In return, I was able to learn more about other parts of the country.

I think about someone like Brian Copeland, who had blonde hair and blue eyes. I was always wondering was what gonna happen to him cause he took on challenges. He got involved in the community activities, and started playing dominoes with guys from the Lower Nine. Before he left, he had bought him a set of dominoes. It really became a people's thing. Young people would come visit this site, and on the return trip, they would bring their parents to see the museum and to meet me. Brian's parents came down to work on the site. It's an honor that someone would think that much of you that they wanted their parents to meet you.

When these young people were getting ready to go on with their life, it was like having my empty nest again, because they became my children. As they all went off one by one, I felt a little mushy,

but I got them all to leave me something, to keep that connection—whether it's Melody Jacobsen's famous black shorts, or the tennis shoes, or the big wooden guitar, or a cap, I still have that connection with these kids. Their picture hangs over my desk with the rest of my friends and family.

Tall Order

Kristyna Filipkova was from the Czech Republic. She was pretty, she was funny, and she would take on any challenge. I remember I was running a jackhammer, and she said, "Ronald Lewis, you don't have to do that. I can do this." I said, "Tall Order, I can handle it," but she would take that jackhammer and put the men on the property to shame.

Contact sheet taken at the House of Dance & Feathers photo shoot by Aubrey Edwards, a professional photographer who came to New Orleans after Katrina to offer her services. Her intent, she says, was to provide "free portraits to New Orleans rebuilders during the aftermath of the storm. The idea behind the project was to document the period of reconstruction in one of America's greatest cities, replace photographs lost in the storm, as well as to give the community a cathartic break from the rebuilding process to pose for a portrait."

Sarah Gamble [*in the University of Florida t-shirt*] was working on the House of Dance & Feathers as part of her job with CITYBuild, a design/build consortium, and saw a listing Aubrey posted on Craigslist. She thought the Tupelo Street worksite would be an ideal candidate for the project. Sarah says, "By that point in the summer, we had fully embraced our construction worker personas. Our nine to five jobs made us increasingly comfortable with each other and our work. Just before this photograph was taken, we inserted a huge picture window into the side of the house [*see opposite page*] that we got at the Green Project, a local store for recycled and salvaged materials. It required an enormous amount of work—sanding, patching, and painting—to get it ready."

The photo shoot used the newly installed window to frame the pictures. The people inside the frame, Sarah says, include "a mix of locals, short-term residents, and relocated post-Katrina rebuilders. Our construction team was constantly changing with members coming in and out each week. Annette, Brian, Caitlin, Melody, and Kyle, the core of the Kansas State University student team, were joined by students like Tomas, Noah, and Kristyna from other schools. Keith and Arnold (aka Urenky), our electricians, joined us halfway through the summer. Charles, our youngest team member, fit construction in between football practice and dominoes." Looking back at that day, Aubrey recalls, "It was the most amazing experience to see them put their tools down, dust themselves off, and sit still and simply smile—if only for a few flashes before getting back to work."

The Royal Tile Cutter

Lucy Begg was on a Branner Traveling Fellowship from the Architecture Department of University of California, Berkeley, experimenting with different forms of community participation in architectural practice. Before arriving in New Orleans, her research grant took her to Berlin, Rome, and London, where she worked on collaborative urban projects. "All the projects I studied, including the House of Dance & Feathers, promoted the civic value of play and performance in public space and the ways in which they can strengthen community ties."

At the worksite, Lucy volunteered to lay tile in the house. Ronald says, "She really got into laying the tile. She was English, and the English are known to put titles to everything, so I started calling her the 'Royal Tile Cutter.' When Lucy left, she made a drawing as a gift to Ronald. Describing what's to be found in the picture, Lucy says, "It's a mishmash of the buildings, personalities, stories, food, and eccentric objects that occupied that site over the summer. There is a big sunflower in one corner for the flowers that were planted, supposedly to suck excess toxins from the soil. Rumor was that they should have been disposed of just before they

bloomed but no one seemed motivated to remove the blaze of yellow optimism. It was only on one of my final days that Ronald confessed quietly that he couldn't wait to be rid of them. He felt unable to express that sentiment publicly because everyone else was enjoying them so much!

"Herbert Gettridge, the 83-year-old master plasterer, is up a ladder working on the house. He was single-handedly renovating his house on the neighboring block at the same time. Watching him put his tools to work was a poetic experience. There is also Ronald's gatekeeper staff with the skull atop it, which he found under the house after almost everything else had been washed away. I included patterns from Ronald's beadwork at the bottom, as well as the Rib-Shack—the trailer in the wrecked Church's Chicken parking lot where we ate lunch every day. There is a barbershop pole and scissors under the Tupelo Street (For Life!) sign, in reference to the informal business Ronald's son ran out of the old museum. What I like about the drawing now is that it encourages you to try and remember more. And when I look at it now, I am reminded of a thousand other things I should have included, too."

A display of "The Katrina Story," an exhibition Ronald put together from newspaper clippings and other media that came out about New Orleans after the storm. In the forefront are cans of water distributed by the Federal Emergency Management Agency (FEMA). Photograph by Devin Meyers of Fotos for Humanity.

People were just riding around the Ninth Ward, looking at this tragedy, this loss that everybody suffered, and this little house on Tupelo Street became the hot thing.

It drew people from around the city and really around the country. Every day, people would come in here. They were crying—they were happy, they were sad. One of the key statements was, "I'm glad that somebody's doing something." It meant a lot to the people to come here and watch. So many people came back to just nothing, this was a feel good place.

Once I got attuned to all the media, scholars, schools, and volunteer groups who were traveling through my neighborhood, I utilized those resources for the benefit of my community—putting that message out there, and letting it be known that the city wasn't gonna tear down our houses and turn our land into "green space." Steve Inskeep ran a series until I moved back home. Then he went on the airwaves and said, "Well, Ronald Lewis is back in his house."

A lot of times in my interviews with people, they will say, "Ronald, you're the exception." I'm not the exception. No, I'm not. Even with me, they don't look at my history as a union organizer. A shop steward. My job was a streetcar track repairman, but I was a professional person in the union. You can talk to people but you can't control how they are going to represent you. One thing that I resented was us being called the poor, poor people of the Lower Ninth Ward, because this community was built off of working class people, and we had our way of life down here that was going

National Public Radio's Morning Edition's crew interviews Ronald at the construction site for the new House of Dance & Feathers. Media coverage often leads to other connections. In Ronald's case, his stories with Steve Inskeep led to a working relationship with *New Yorker* writer Dan Baum. Working on a long piece for the magazine, Dan says, he "found Ronald the way most reporters did; through other journalists' work—in this case, from listening to him talk on NPR. He and I drove out to his Tupelo Street house in January 2006. It was five months since Katrina, but the Lower Nine was a sodden wasteland. Ronald stood on the dead grass in front of his ruined house and described how everybody in the neighborhood was going to come back. I remember thinking, 'This poor man has been out in the hot sun too long.' To my eyes, the Lower Nine was finished. Ronald, though, saw what few others saw, and, of course, he turned out to be right." When Dan began working on a book about New Orleans, he decided to make Ronald one of his main characters. The weeks they spent together recording Ronald's story can be found in *Nine Lives: Death and Life in New Orleans* from Spiegel & Grau. Photograph by Caitlin Heckathorn.

to help us come back. In the first story Dan Baum wrote for the *New Yorker* magazine, he said he felt sorry for me because he didn't know when I was gonna come back to reality. I told him, "Dan, you're a journalist, and you can't look and feel what I was feeling, and you did what a journalist do." Now he calls me Prophet Lewis and is a key advocate for this community through his writing because he's seen the spirit of the people of this Lower Ninth Ward.

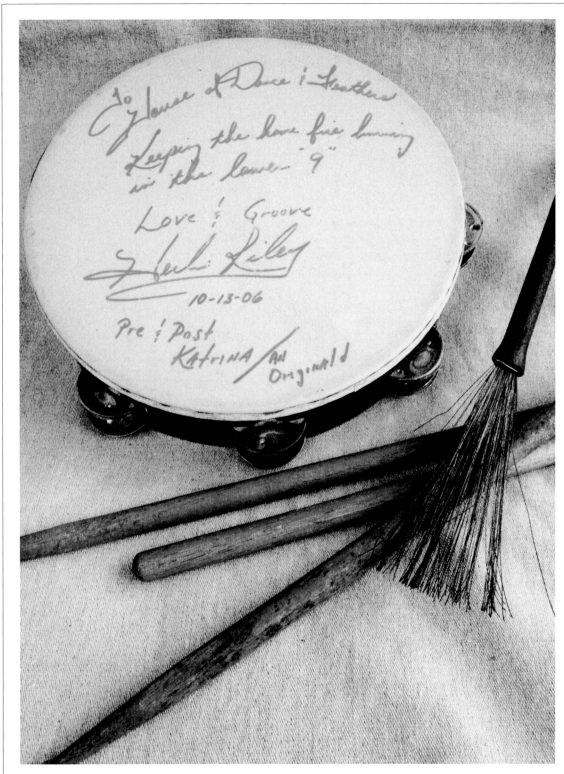

Tambourine and drumsticks donated to the museum by Herlin Riley, Jr., who grew up in the Lower Ninth Ward and is a drummer at Lincoln Center in New York City. Herlin's message reads: "To House of Dance & Feathers, Keeping the home fire burning in the lower '9.' Love & Groove, Herlin Riley 10-13-06 Pre & Post Katrina/An Original." Photograph by Devin Meyers of Fotos for Humanity.

Top: The grand opening of the House of Dance & Feathers in August of 2006. Photograph by Jason Fedak. *Right:* Ronald leading a tour at the newly opened museum. Photograph by Patrick Rhodes.

Reopening

Curating the new museum is like making an Indian suit. Each suit develops its own life, and the new House of Dance & Feathers is creating its new identity. There are no domino games, no haircutting, and all the stories are being told by me. It's my museum, but it's for the people. When you become too restrictive, then it has no meaning.

Left: Darryl Keys, the Second Chief of the Comanche Hunters from the Lower Ninth Ward, donated the pair of shoes he wore during Mardi Gras 2006. Darryl shares the story of how the shoes ended up in the museum: "The Comanche Hunters was the first gang from the Lower Ninth Ward to mask after Katrina. It was just me, my two cousins—Vernon Freeman and Jonathan Molton—and two little Queens. They were living in FEMA trailers and I had rented a house in the Seventh Ward. We said, 'We're gonna all chip in and do it.'

"Most people weren't gonna mask or come back for carnival because they lost their homes. Why mask? I decided to do it for the people. While everyone was in Texas and all over the world, I was sitting at home sewing. A lot of my patches, brooches, and materials in my attic never got wet in the storm—they were dirty, but salvageable. When I saw the patch

In the third year after Katrina, Lori Waselchuk photographed Percy Francois, Lil Chief of the Comanche Hunters, crossing the North Claiborne Avenue Bridge in 2008. The image is part of a series, "Love and Concrete," that explores the North Claiborne corridor from the Sixth Ward to the Lower Ninth Ward. Lori says, "I continue to think about New Orleans as an island: its bridges standing irresolutely as either a link or a barrier to the rest of Louisiana and the country."

on my old boots, I felt like I wanted to make new pair, but then I said, 'No, I'm going to let people see the dirt. They survived the storm.' The original boots were blue, but I took the patches off and chose red material for the people who died in the storm.

"The day we paraded, we went back in the Lower Ninth Ward. We said a prayer by the barge that broke through the levee and then we started walking up Claiborne to the St. Claude Bridge, singing two songs we made up—'Busted Levee' and 'How You Gon' Cross the Water.' You got to cross the bridge to get to and from our neighborhood. A lot of people were sitting on that bridge during the storm and had no food, no water. And the bridge was up, so they couldn't cross.

"That day I walked through the Ninth Ward, across the bridge, all the way to Shakespeare Park in the muddy shoes that went through Katrina, I felt like nothing could stop me. If Katrina couldn't stop

these shoes, nothing could. I wanted to donate those. A patch is something on your body but the shoes—walking through the Ninth Ward—means a lot.

"I told Mr. Ronald to never clean them because you'll take the royalty out of it. It's like if you find old money—don't clean it because you lose the value of it. These shoes are straight off the land." Photograph by Devin Meyers of Fotos for Humanity.

Louisiana
INDIANS

Part III

The beginnings of a beaded patch by Ronald W. Lewis. Photograph by Devin Meyers of Fotos for Humanity.

Mardi Gras Indians

Left: Joe Scott's work table on the porch of the FEMA trailer that Edgar Jacobs, Big Chief of the Choctaw Hunters, has been living in since Katrina. *Right:* Derrick Magee works on a patch for his 2009 suit. Photographs by Rachel Breunlin.

Mardi Gras Indians

By Rachel Breunlin

"Africa introduces a different art history, a history of danced art, defined in the blending of movement and sculpture, textiles, and other forms." —Robert Farris Thompson[1]

"This was one of the biggest feats that ever happened during the Mardi Gras in New Orleans. Even when the parades that cost millions of dollars would be coming along, if a band of Indians was coming, why the parade wouldn't have anybody there. Everybody would flock to see the Indians. They would dance, and they would sing, and they would go on just like the regular Indians." —Jelly Roll Morton[2]

When the doors to the House of Dance & Feathers opened again, the stories about the neighborhood-based groups of Black, working class New Orleanians who spend most of the year sewing elaborate Indian suits to wear on Mardi Gras day once again became central to the museum. Their history is deeply tied to the history of southern Louisiana, a region of the "New World" that was formed through the violent yet formative cultural exchanges among European, African, and indigenous peoples.[3] Their debut on the streets of New Orleans comes at a critical point in U.S. racial policies. The writer Kalamu ya Salaam, who grew up in the Lower Ninth Ward, writes, "Like blues, jazz, and other deeply rooted examples of African American culture, 'Injuns' (as neighborhood people affectionately refer to them) date back to the post reconstruction era...a significant period of racist repression and outright terror."[4] At a time when direct political confrontation was increasingly dangerous, masking as Indian became a Black carnival tradition

One of the important components of a Mardi Gras Indian suit is the headdress, known as a "crown." When comparing photographs of American Indian headdresses with early Mardi Gras Indian crowns, the similarities are striking. *Left:* An historical photo of an American Indian wearing a war bonnet with beaded brow band, courtesy of Written Heritage, Folsom, Louisiana. *Center:* A *wapaha,* a Lakota Feathered Headdress, from 1954 in a more modern style decorated with eagle feathers. Photographs courtesy of The Buechel Memorial Lakota Museum [5] at St. Francis Mission, St. Francis, South Dakota. *Right:* A Mardi Gras Indian in the 1940s, by Homer Turner, courtesy of the Historic New Orleans Collection. Turner's image shows a similar beaded brow band to the historical photograph of the "war bonnet."

The use of feathers in Mardi Gras Indian suits may have other sources of inspiration besides Plains Indians. When African art historian Robert Farris Thompson showed photographs of Mardi Gras Indians to Fu-Kiau Bunseki, the founder of the Kongo Academy in Kumba in Bas-Zaire, Bunseki emphasized the importance of feathers in masking amongst the Bakongo in Central Africa. In Thompson's summary of the possible pan-African links, he says, "Feathers on masks or headdresses in Kongo are medicines, referring to confidence and strength built into the vaunting of the power to fly. They teach that it is possible to cure illness by rising out of ourselves, emerging from our physical situation into full spiritual awareness and potentiality. Then, by means of radiant sky-implying feathers, heaven can speak of cures we need." [6]

that spoke to both historical and contemporary struggles for freedom.

Ronald says, "Coming out of slavery, being African American wasn't socially acceptable. By masking like Native Americans, it created an identity of strength. The Native Americans, under all the pressure and duress, would not concede. These people were almost drove into extinction to maintain their way of life. And the same kind of feeling, coming out slavery, 'You're not going giving us a place here in society, we'll create our own.' In masking, they paid respect and homage to the Native American for using their identity and making a social statement that despite the odds, you're still not going to stop."

Left: Jewelry worn by Leroy Ross, Flagboy of the White Cloud Hunters Mardi Gras tribe, including a ring with the image of an American Indian with a headdress he had made in a jewelry store in New Orleans. Photograph by Rachel Breunlin. *Center:* Vernon Freeman, Flagboy of the Comanche Hunters, holding beaded patches he is working on at the House of Dance & Feathers. Photograph by Rachel Breunlin. *Right:* Darryl Keys, Second Chief of the Comanche Hunters in 2006, wearing a beaded patch with American Indian imagery. Photograph by Elliott Hammer.

Questions Around Origin

There are two origin stories for Mardi Gras Indians in New Orleans. The first, put forward by Michael P. Smith in his book *Mardi Gras Indians*, asserts that the rise of African Americans masking as Indians occurred around the arrival of Buffalo Bill's Wild West show in New Orleans in 1884–85. Smith points to the use of Plains Indian imagery in the suits and to the name of the first tribe on record, the Creole Wild West.[7] Lil Walter Cook, Big Chief of the tribe, disputes this claim, arguing that oral histories passed down in his family trace their involvement in the masking tradition to at least the 1830s.[8]

Like Lil Walter, many other New Orleanians who mask Indian prefer to emphasize the historical connections between Africans and Indian tribes in the area, pointing to the history of intermarriage in Louisiana and often claiming indigenous heritage themselves. There are a number of laws that, historically, made these connections hard to claim explicitly. In the "Acts and Records of the Cabildo" from 1781, the Attorney General declared,

all kinds of masking, the wearing of feathers, gathering at the local taverns, and public dancing by the negroes be prohibited this carnival season.[9]

The decree speaks to the fact that people of African descent were already using feathers well before the Buffalo Bill show arrived. Another law, spoken about at length by Reverend Goat Carson in *Tootie's Last Suit*, is the Indian Removal Act of 1830, which made it dangerous to identify directly with local tribes for fear of displacement to Oklahoma.[10]

When asked about their history, most Mardi Gras Indians agree that they are honoring Indians for their resistance to U.S. invasion, their support of African Americans, and their ability to hold on to their culture under policies of forced assimilation. In beaded patches, many of the images tell stories of Native American history that often have a secondary, more contemporary meaning for indigenous and African American struggles. For instance, Alonzo Moore, Wildman of the Ninth Ward Navajo, beaded an American Indian praying on top of a mountain as part of his 2006 suit to symbolize his hope that people would come home after Hurricane Katrina. Outside of masking for

The beading traditions amongst the Yoruba and Plains Indians also come from a convergence of cross-cultural influences. *Left:* A beaded crown of the king, known as the Ajalorun, of Ijebu-Ife, Ijebu-Yoruba. Historically, glass beads were imported from medieval Europe and Islamic trade routes, and were possibly made locally at commmercial centers such as Ile-Ife as well.[16] Wearing beadwork in Yorubaland represents status and rank. As African art historian Henry John Drewal writes, "Beads distinguish their owners and alert the viewer to matters of position, knowledge, and power."[17] Photograph courtesy of Henry John Drewal.

In Mardi Gras Indian tribes, designing and beading a more elaborate crown is a way to gain more recognition, and possibly a more prestigious position within the gang. Amongst the Yoruba, beaded regalia is commissioned by royalty who wear them as a symbol of their inner spiritual head—the artwork representative of power they already have rather than what they were able to achieve from the labor and art of beading.[18]

In most Plains Indian tribes, beadwork is done by women, and the designs often came from dreams that were important gifts from the spirit world. *Right:* This beaded horse mask, made in 1998 by Joyce Growing Thunder (Assiniboine/ Sioux, born 1950), is made with similar materials to those used during the 1800s, the era when Black New Orleanians were said to be inspired by their work. At the time, "traders had only recently brought Venetian glass seed beads to the Plains," which had sparked a new style of artwork that lifted Plains artwork to "its zenith."[19] Photograph courtesy of the artist.

carnival, many Mardi Gras Indians wear jewelry and collect memorabilia and books to deepen their connection to their own tradition as well as their solidarity with indigenous people.[11]

The Backstreet Cultural Museum, with the support of Reverend Goat Carson, a Christian minister and a shaman of Cherokee descent, have also reached out to American Indian nations. In 2003, members of Fi Yi Yi visited the Cheyenne River Reservation of the Lakota Nation at the invitation of Chief Arval Looking Horse.[12] In 2007, the Backstreet received a grant from the National Endowment for the Arts to put together a cultural exchange program between Mardi Gras Indians and the Hopi, Navajo, and Apache Nations. It also supports White Buffalo Day at Congo Square, an event that brings together Mardi Gras Indian tribes and members of Indian nations.[13]

Patchwork

Since its beginnings, masking as a Mardi Gras Indian has developed into an elaborate art form.

The beadwork, held to increasingly high standards by the tribes, has been recognized by national institutions.[14] With the recognition has come many attempts to trace the cultural and artistic roots. In the catalogue to Allison "Tootie" Montana's exhibition at the New Orleans Museum of Art, *He's the Prettiest*, African art curator Bill Fagaly writes,

> Without a doubt the century-old tradition. . . reminiscent of the American Plain Indian dress and the beadwork of Yoruba peoples of Nigeria ranks high in our city's unique contribution to American culture. It too has associations which stem from Africa by way of the Caribbean.[15]

Like in New Orleans, an identification with indigenous people in ritual performances as well as sophisticated beading in artwork can be found across the Caribbean. In Haitian town of Léogane, Rara season is called an "Indian festival." Cultural anthropologist Elizabeth McAlister says the processions are "fleeting yearly remembrance

Throughout carnival and Lent in Haiti, groups take to the street for spiritual, political, and social empowerment. *Left:* A painting by the Haitian artist Wilson Bigaud depicts a Mardi Gras Indian in Port-au-Prince. The *Edeyen Madigra* costumes are strikingly similar in size and aesthetic to Mardi Gras Indians of New Orleans, especially the echo of the American Indian headdress. The shield-shaped tunics of the New Orleans and Haitian Indians, as well as the Rara costume, are similar to Catholic priests' chasubles, Yoruban vestments, and even Masonic aprons. All shine elaborately with beads, braiding, and sequins.

On Ash Wednesday, the Raras begin gathering their own groups. A hierarchy is chosen, sequin artists design and start sewing, and musicians play handmade instruments. Lenten preparations and promenades culminate in three days of continuous performance from Good Friday through Easter Sunday. *Right:* Luc Cedor [*sitting*], an *oüngan*, or Vodou priest, who heads Rara Azaka (St. Isador), performs a blessing on Good Friday before the parades begin. Photographs courtesy of Tina Girouard.[25]

of the 250,000 Tainos who died in the first few years after Columbus' fateful 1492 arrival in Haiti."[20] Participants dress in elaborately beaded sequined costumes reminiscent of vodou flags.[21] In Trinidad, the Lakota spiritual leader, Black Elk, is honored by an Afro-Trinidadian carnival group called the House of Black Elk. Each year, members parade in meticulously researched and recreated costumes reminiscent of North American Plains Indians in the mid-to-late 1800s.[22]

In addition to the beading, there are other similarities in performance traditions between New Orleans and the Caribbean. Junkanoo groups, who are part of the year-end and holiday festivities in the West Indies, are one example. Like Mardi Gras Indians, they "form fierce allegiances and followings. During their processions, they pull their supporters into their performances with call-and-response chants and strong percussion upheld with tambourines, cowbells, washboards, bottles and sticks."[23] Music is blended with dance and art to create multi-sensory experiences that performance scholars call "theater in life" events.[24]

What's Ahead

Much of the literature on Mardi Gras Indians includes sensitive discussions of the sensory layers involved in their performances, including the artistry of the suits, the tribal structure, the songs and dance that accompany different positions, and the ritual meetings of gangs at practices and on the street. These accounts, however, often talk in the abstract, and rarely give a sense of the particulars of individual and group experiences and creativity.

Ronald's narrative, along with extended captions from people represented in the catalogue, provides these details by telling personal stories that build on (and influence) the broader cultural history. The subsections roughly follow a timeline around Ronald's involvement in sewing, but also speak to the larger trends in the community.

While most of the literature emphasizes the importance of "sewing one's own suit," the reality is actually much more interesting. As Jeffrey David Ehrenreich writes, "The work is an intersection of individuals with their communities."[26]

There are Indians who pride themselves on sewing their own, while other tribes work together, almost like a guild, to create them. Some people have spent decades working on suits without ever masking themselves. Historically, the sewing was done as labors of love amongst close-knit groups of friends. These days, the situation can be more complicated. As money circulates from New Orleans Jazz & Heritage Festival gigs, as well as other performances, recordings, and the sale of suits, some sewers expect to be paid for their services.

Throughout the book, Mardi Gras Indians' commitment to their neighborhoods and tribal lineages are important overriding themes. Many tribes, such as the Wild Magnolias or Ninth Ward Hunters, have explicit ties to neighborhoods, while others trace their roots back to certain areas through particular mentors and sewing traditions.

The histories of tribes follow different pathways through the city, as people involved in the culture may have moved, changed tribes, or started their own. Many people continue to mask where their tribe was established and to honor the history and relationships that were developed there. For that reason, where a tribe comes out may not necessarily correlate with where the Big Chief is currently living. Lil Walter Cook, for instance, lives in the Lower Ninth Ward, but comes out with his tribe at his mother's beauty salon in Central City. Similarly, Victor Harris, the Big Chief of Fi Yi Yi, lives in the Ninth Ward, but comes out where he grew up in the Seventh Ward on Annette Street. Both gangs have developed strong followings in the neighborhoods

where they first began masking. Like other gangs, when they take to the streets, their group of supporters will be waiting. Each year, the combination of people might be slightly different. The supporters include Indians who aren't masking that year, people who helped sew the suits or provided other resources and support, and others who have made a lifelong commitment to participating however they can—people like Tyrone Miller, who never masked himself but made a contribution to the culture through music. Big Chief Ronald "Buck" Baham remembers, "He loved the Indians and no one could sing 'Shoo Fly' like he did. When the song begins, everyone backs up. They let him sing it alone." The following pages attempt to give a sense of the complex network of people that keep the performance tradition a vibrant part of the backstreets of New Orleans.

Tyrone Miller [*in wheelchair*] sings with the Seventh Ward Warriors in front of the Backstret Cultural Museum on Mardi Gras Day in 2005. Photograph by Rachel Breunlin.

Opposite page: Issac "Ike" Edwards and Bob Bertrand of the White Eagles Mardi Gras Indian tribe. Born on May 1, 1923, Mr. Ike grew up on Philip Street between Willow and Clara. He started masking in 1932. He remembers, "I came up masking under Brother Tilman, the Big Chief of the Creole Wild West. He was mixed with Indian from Houma, Louisiana. He taught me how to sew. We used to go to the junk store and find evening gowns and use a razor blade to take the beads and sequins off. We took pretty earrings, too. We used canvas for our aprons. We put satin over old vests from three-piece suits, and sewed the beads on them. To make the crowns, we found our feathers at neighborhood groceries selling live turkeys during Thanksgiving. We boiled water with a dye called Tintex and dropped the feathers in to get the color we wanted."

Back then, Indians masked throughout the year. Mr. Ike remembers, "We could put our suits on any time. For Halloween or St. Joseph's night, we'd carry lanterns and walk to the Dew Drop Inn and corner barrooms, or we'd go in a truck to the Tulane Club or the San Jacinto." When Brother Tilman started getting older, Mr. Ike and some of the other Indians like Wildman Herman, Robert "Robbe" Lee, and Lawrence Fletcher from the Creole Wild West joined the Golden Blades, and then formed their own gang, the White Eagles. They sewed at a barroom at Josephine and Magnolia called Bob's Playhouse. After a while, the owner, Bob Bertrand, "decided to he wanted to be a part of us. On Sundays, he used to ride horses. He had a lot back in Zion City and that's where he kept them. Clarence Fletcher borrowed one of his horses for carnival. He was one of the first to come out on a horse doing an Indian thing. He just wanted to do something different."

The photo of Mr. Ike and Mr. Bob was taken at Abadie Studio in Central City after carnival in 1952. During that time, the Black run studio was where everyone in the uptown neighborhood went for photographs. Mr. Ike had been an Indian for 20 years. It was the last year he masked. Photograph donated to the museum by Ray "Hatchet" Blazio, who was introduced to Mr. Ike by Wilbur Yancy after Big Chief Donald Harrison Senior's funeral.

A Lifetime Addiction

Ricky Gettridge, former Spyboy of the Yellow Pocahontas Mardi Gras Indian gang, playing the tambourine as the YPH parades through the Seventh Ward. He remembers his early years in the neighborhood, when Indian practice was held in the yard next door to his house. "It's the first house I knew. I could remember the Wildman had me crying my eyes out on that corner. I was scared to death of those Indians then."

When his family moved to the Ninth Ward in the late 1950s—first to the Desire Public Housing Development and then to the Lower Ninth Ward—his father still masked with the YPH. Ricky himself masked as a Spyboy for six years in bold color schemes like red and white diamonds, pink and black, orchid and orange. Although he stopped masking, he never stopped sewing. "After that, I offered my assistance. I always felt good to help any and everybody who would be serious about this. Even a stranger—I liked to inspire and see it happen. Not just the YPH but the neighboring tribes all over the Sixth Ward, the Seventh Ward—all over the Ninth Ward. I've helped start plenty of them and some became better than me. They were students of mine. I helped birth them into the game, and I was there to cheer them on—to assist them, sing with them, and meet the other gangs." Photograph by Jeffrey David Ehrenreich.

When you hear the hum of the people talking about, "That person is a Mardi Gras Indian," you know that person is very special. Everybody don't do it.

I used to work at a little neighborhood grocery in the mid-1960s called Money Savers. Ricky Gettridge came by the store one day and said, "Well, Ronald, I'm masking. Come by my house." He lived on Tennessee Street near the St. Claude Bridge in the Lower Ninth Ward. We went to middle school together. I went over not knowing that I was going to end up with a lifetime addiction to the thread and needle.

Ricky's daddy, Merlin Gettridge, masked with Allison "Tootie" Montana, the Big Chief of the Yellow Pocahontas (YPH). The YPH were from the hub of the Seventh Ward, where there were lots of craftsmen who worked with their hands—bricklayers, cement finishers, ironworkers, lathers like Tootie, and plasterers like Ricky's daddy, Spyboy Hoppy. They transferred those skills of their labor to their costumes.[27]

Left: Fred Johnson as Spyboy of the Yellow Pocahontas [*with Tootie Montana behind him in powder blue*]. Photograph by Ronald W. Lewis. *Right:* Franklin "Wingy" Davis. While there are usually many significant moments that lead up to a decision to mask, the final catalyst occured for Wingy when he was parading with the Bucket Men, a club that a lot of YPH Indians were in. He recalls, "Fred Johnson told me, 'Man, you don't want to fool with that—it's like a drug addiction. You can't get it out of you.' I drew my first pictures and told the guys, 'It's not for second lines, it's for Indians.' The guys said, 'We usually help the newcomers, but it's too late this year.' I told them I started already. They were impressed: 'You did this all by yourself?' I did my sewing with guidance from Melvin Reed and Jerome Smith. Fred and I, we ran double Spyboy. That's where all the fun was. Our suits were lighter and smaller because we were active—we literally ran up and down the tribe, letting the members know what's going on ahead. If you're good, you'll know what tribe it is five or six blocks away. Your chief will know before he ever sees a feather." Photograph of Wingy donated by Melvin Reed.

The design of Ricky's suit was a fighting kite, and he gave me this flower design to sew. As a Yellow Pocahontas, he used sequins and beads. They were the hardest things in the world to pick up. You got to pick up the sequins first, and then you pick up the bead, then you loop over and go back under with the thread. It becomes repetitious, and you're talking about thousands and thousands of these itty-bitty things. That one design took me as long to sew as it took the family to put together a whole suit!

From my start with middle school, the urge just heightened about the Mardi Gras Indian culture. It has mystique to it. Curiosity.

Over the years, I got to know some of the greatest Mardi Gras Indians who ever wore a suit, and not just the YPH family, but other Mardi Gras Indians, too, like Walter Cook, Senior, who had the greatest stories about making these suits and creating an identity. He had such a simple way of telling you about masking. He'd tell us, "Do your best and then when that day comes, wear your suit and don't worry about what you didn't get done." He talked more about the people who were the chiefs of certain gangs, and how proud the men were. I was like a child in a candy store, just absorbing everything that he offered.

Beadwork by Ricky Gettridge for Rashad "Fat" Lewis' crown. This beadwork was worn in 1990, but the beading tradition it comes out of is more than 50 years old. Ricky says, "My daddy taught me how to sew in this style of stonework. Place the stone, thread the needle. There is a hole in each side of the rhinestone. The center one in this picture has four holes. You come up from the bottom, go over the edges and back down a couple of times for durability. To make it stationary. Then you shield it with sequins and beads to come up with different layers."

Henry John Drewal, who has studied the work of master beaders for years, found that "the act of beading requires intense concentration and small-scale, delicate repetitive action—something that makes time pass without notice and causes the eyes to go out of focus, blurring one's vision and creating a dream-like state. The gestures of beading begin to take over, to have their own momentum, life, and energy with which the beader is in synchrony. Beading is thus a physical as well as a metaphysical experience in which artists become both masters of and mastered by their medium." [28] Photograph by Devin Meyers of Fotos for Humanity.

Big Chief Lil Walter Cook of the Creole Wild West and Allison "Tootie" Montana of the Yellow Pocahontas. Photograph by Ronald W. Lewis.

I started seeking out people that said they were masking. I helped people sew. From sewing, you learn how to decorate, you learn how to design, and after a while you become an integral part of the society. It's a family. When you're sewing, everybody gets on the same page. You're sharing in those old war stories, and there's a ritual of having refreshment: beans cooked and hot dogs. It becomes an event in itself.

As you get older and get more experience in making the suits, you pick up a visionary thing about the beads. You can almost count how many beads go in a certain spot. It's like an artist with a brush who gets his stroke and flow into his painting. You get the feel in your hands, in your eyes, and your juices just flow. In the year of making a suit, you may go through numerous hardships and distractions. The sewing become a meditation. Your focus is only on what you working on. It's therapy, really.

Opposite page: Darryl Montana, Big Chief of the Yellow Pocahontas Mardi Gras Indian tribe, wearing a suit dedicated to his
father, Allison "Tootie" Montana, in 2006. The apron of the suit
was an image of Tootie in the last suit he made before he passed.
Photograph by Jeffrey David Ehrenreich.

Three-Dimensional Creative Designs

*A Mardi Gras Indian is one of the
best clothing designers there is.*

From sleeveless vests to full jackets, to crowns
with turkey feathers to plumes, as people become
innovators in building bigger and better mouse-
traps, they develop new styles. There are two
major styles of sewing—three-dimensional creative designs and pictoral beadwork. These styles
are associated with different parts of the city—
downtown and uptown—but they aren't locked to
geography. Depending on where an Indian moves
during his lifetime, where relatives and friends
live who are involved in masking, who taught him
or her how to sew, and what styles the person is
interested in, they might sew in an uptown style
while masking downtown or vice versa. Others
might combine elements for a new look.

The battles are won through the thread and needle. You always want to follow your Indian to
battle to see the response of the people, but at the
same time, you want to see what other individuals have done that year. Mardi Gras Indians are
similar to architects. When an architect designs
work behind another architect, that's a compli-
ment. Once we see a Mardi Gras Indian who has
incorporated something new into his suit, we
might take over it to see what kind of effect you
can get out of it, too—not as a copycat, but as an
appreciation of that person's suit.

Years ago, most of the headdresses, which we call
crowns, were done with turkey feathers. They called
them mummy crowns because they were very tall
and weren't that flexible. This style is still popular—
especially in the Sixth, Seventh, and Eighth
Wards—but it's gone through changes, too.

Melvin Reed, at his house on New Orleans Street, goes through
photographs of Indian suits he helped design and sew. Growing up
on N. Villere and Pauger in the Seventh Ward, Melvin was in the
middle of the neighborhood's sewing culture. He says, "I'm good
with the hands. I looked at some of the suits Montana made—
how he made shapes out of cardboard—and taught myself how to
sew. I designed with Fred Johnson, Stacy Banks, and Ray Blazio.
I designed the first suit Victor Harris ever wore with Fi Yi Yi,
before he switched to an African style."

When Melvin moved to Gentilly he still continued to sew for the
Yellow Pocahontas. "I worked at Swiss Bakery as a cake decorator,
and would come home and sew until two or three in the morning.
One year, nine Indian suits came out of this house. The cats who
sit down and discuss schemes and designs for suits always tell me, 'I
was in Reed's school.'" Photograph by Rachel Breunlin.

Top: Ray "Hatchet" Blazio wearing a peacock suit for his position as Flagboy for the Yellow Pocahontas. He tells a little of his history of masking. "In 1952, when I was 12 years old, this fella Charles Farria, the Flagboy for the Monogram Hunters, took a liking to me and said he would make me a suit for carnival. He didn't finish in time, but I got to wear it for St. Joseph's Night. I went with the Monogram Hunters to dance at the San Jacinto Club in Tremé. They had a gang of Indians from uptown and downtown, and I met Lawrence Fletcher, the Big Chief of the White Eagles. He was clowning with me to see what I knew and I did my little dance. After that night, I couldn't wait to do it on my own.

"I masked with Tootie from 1961 to 1969. He drew all my designs, and I got a lot of pointers from Jerome Smith, too. Tootie's Queen, Ms. Ruby, was Jerome Smith's auntie and nannan [*godmother*], and Jerome liked to come around and help Tootie sew. Over time, he showed me how to make my suits better, too.

"When Jerome joined the Congress on Racial Equality (CORE), he was on the road a lot, but always came back for carnival. In 1964, I decided to make a peacock suit because it's a beautiful bird and its colors sit pretty on the white. Jerome and my companion at the time, Viola Emelian, helped me sew it."

Bottom: Ray Blazio wearing a peacock suit as the Big Chief of the Wild Apaches. He explains, "The Wild Apaches started because of bunch of guys from the neighborhood were interested in masking. My friend Huey Journee, who we call Boss, told me, 'I want to mask before I die,' and that's what made me come back. I was Big Chief for a few years, and then Wingy took over. In 2000, I came back with the peacock design. Pernell Butler and Wilbur Yancy helped with the suit." Photographs donated by Ray Blazio.

Ray "Hatchet" Blazio
Big Chief of the Wild Apaches

I met Ray Blazio, better known as Hatchet, through Ricky Gettridge when he was masking with YPH. Hatchet was the Flagboy and he was renowned at his position. He masked consistently until the late 1960s, and then quit masking. When Hatchet came back on the streets, he started a gang with another YPH alumni, Franklin "Wingy" Davis, and came back as the Big Chief of the Wild Apaches in 1991. Tell you what, we have a certain appreciation for those who sit out for so long and decide to come back—that encore—that one more time.

Let me tell you about Mardi Gras Indians. There's a certain suit that they made and years later they felt that that suit wasn't as good as they wanted it to be. Whether it's a color or the design of the suit, they'll come back and say, "Well, man, I know I can wear it better." I've seen them do it time and time again.

Look at Hatchet's original peacock that he wore when he was a Flagboy for the YPH, and look at his most recent peacock, when he was Big Chief. You can see the YPH/downtown influence and how his original concept evolved.

The Big Chief of the Seventh Ward Warriors, Ronald "Buck" Baham, working on his Indian suits. He explains how he sews creative designs: "To make the three–dimensional work, you've got to build up the designs with cardboard—piece by piece. Staple them all together to make sure they fit, then pull them all aloose. You can see on my green suit, the dickey has three different heights. The sides, which we call bridges, are sewn as well. When you have the right sizes, you can glue them together, but you've got to take your time to hold it to make sure the glue is dry before you go onto the next section. Once you have the structure, then you can begin sewing. If you sew it first and then try to build it up, you'll mess up because you'll have exposed pieces of cardboard. I like to bead the seams where the bridges and design meet with pearls."

In addition to the technical side of the craft, creating an Indian suit takes time, patience, and money. Buck says, "You've got to be devoted. Don't be afraid to spend the money to make you a pretty suit because you're not gonna make a pretty suit for a little bit of money. Like me, when I start off and go into the store, whatever colors or rhinestones I'm going to sew with—I don't care how much it is—if I like it, I'm gonna use it. Because I work every day. I buy my stuff. I don't wait for anybody to give me nothing. I've been doing it out of my pocket every year."
Photographs by Rachel Breunlin.

Ronald "Buck" Baham in his green suit. Photograph by Ronald W. Lewis.

Ronald "Buck" Baham
Big Chief of the Seventh Ward Warriors

I started seeing Buck out there on the street, and I just liked something about him. You know, a lot of the Seventh Ward sewing has a story in it—it could be about crawfish, mermaids, dragons.

This particular year, Buck's suit was beautifully sewn with designs, but without images to tell a story.

Lil Charles working on his Indian suit before Katrina. In 2005, he was coming up on 50 years of masking. He began with the Yellow Jackets in 1956. Although his mother's brother, Thomas Sparks, was the Big Chief of the tribe, "my mama couldn't stand Indian. She'd say, 'Get that out of here.' I told her it was fun."

In 1982, after years of running Flagboy for the Yellow Jackets, Lil Charles went to Jake Millon of the White Eagles and Harold Featherson of the White Cloud Hunters asking for their blessing to start his own tribe. He explains, "Two chiefs have to meet and see whether you are responsible enough to be chief. It's more than just making a pretty suit. Do you know how to handle your position?" Retired as Big Chief of the White Cloud Hunters, Harold gave the gang to Lil Charles. Photograph by Joyce Taylor.

Lil Charles Taylor
Big Chief of the White Cloud Hunters

Lil Charles used to work on the waterfront as a sign painter for the Port Authority, but ill health caused him not to be able to work or mask for a few years. Then, in 2008, Lil Charles came out in one of the greatest suits he ever made (and he made some fantastic suits over the years). He's a perfectionist at doing decorations on his suit. In the photograph on the right [*Big Queen Joyce in the front, Big Chief Charles behind her wearing a suit with creative designs*], you can see how his cuffs cascade all the way to the ground. Look at how he got strings of beads popping off the mask. He didn't leave a stone unturned.

The White Cloud Hunters walk down St. Claude towards the Backstreet Museum. After Katrina, Lil Charles says he decided "to build a monster." While in exile in California, his wife, Joyce Taylor, who had never masked before, dreamt that they were coming up Canal Street on Mardi Gras day wearing orange suits. When they returned to New Orleans a few months before carnival, she had the dream again. Inspired, she asked Lil Charles, "Could I be Queen? I want to mask." He said, "Don't make me sew this outfit and then you turn and say you don't want to do it." Joyce was committed, responding, "Oh, I *want.*" Spurred on by an image, "Orange sunshine, shine on me," Lil Charles made her suit from the material remaining from his own—already finished with his wings, he cut out Joyce's dress from the leftover fabric. He recalls standing in the kitchen putting on his boots on Mardi Gras morning. "I turned around and saw Joyce in her suit. I said, 'Oooh! Look at my baby! You look beautiful.' It was shocking to me." Photograph by Jeffrey David Ehrenreich.

Opposite page: Big Chief of the Golden Eagles, Joseph Pierre "Monk" Boudreaux, wearing a crown of ostrich plumes. Monk explains, "The uptown Indians I come from are different from downtown. They mostly use designs and we use pictures. The older people taught me how to sew. My dad, Raymond Boudreaux, was a Flagboy with the Wild Squatoulas and they used to march with the Red, White and Blue. As a kid, I used to help him. When he stopped, I was a runner for the Chief of the White Eagles—I came to the Chief's house to learn and run errands. If he needed thread, I'd go get it. I knew it was something I wanted to do. In order to prove that to the Chief and my dad, I had to sit down and show my commitment."

Monk remembers the first beaded patch he worked on after he was promoted to Chief Scout. "I drew a picture of an Indian standing up with a spear in his hand. When I got halfway finished beading it, I tried to glitter the bottom. My dad and the chief didn't say nothing. *I knew.* I knew it wasn't right but I was pushed for time. I had to go back and do my homework right. From there, I moved up."

As Big Chief of the Golden Eagles, he still draws his own pictures. "I just see something in my mind—people, knives, hatchets, eagles—and get a pencil and paper. Work on it til it's the way I want it. By me being a house painter, I know colors. I'll be looking at a paint chart and I'll take it back to the fabric store and give them a swatch and they'll take it from there. Or sometimes I walk around in a fabric store and look for a color nobody's worn before. The color just pops out at ya." Photograph by Jeffrey David Ehrenreich.

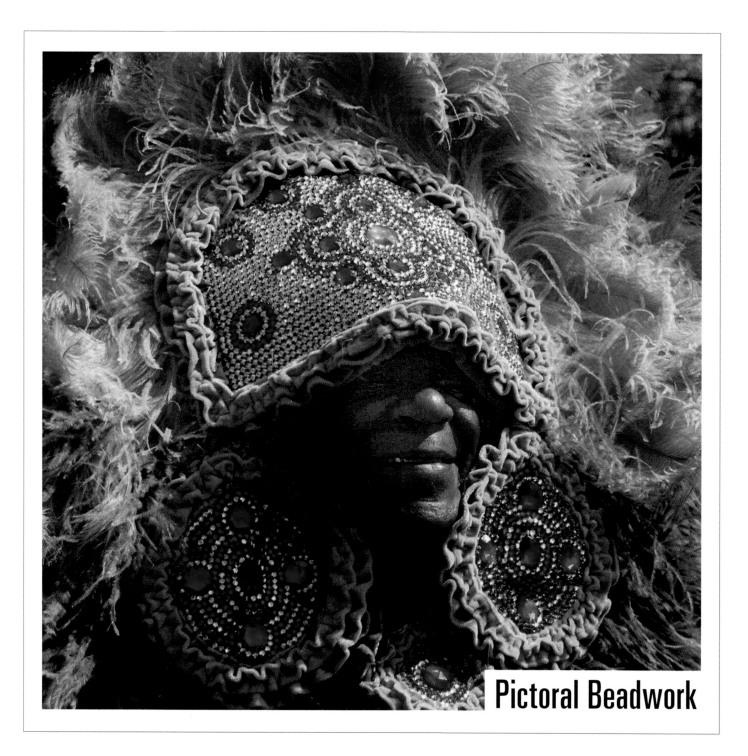

Pictoral Beadwork

Beaded patch by Ronald W. Lewis. Big Chief Lil Walter Cook, who worked with Ronald on Indian suits, explains the standard: "The smaller the bead, the better the patch." Photograph by Beverly Kunze, courtesy of Beverly Kunze Photography.

The Indians uptown have a different style to the creative designs that developed downtown. They sew pictoral beadwork.

In the early days, they used the resources that were available to them—sewing glass, bottle tops, and shells onto sacks to make their aprons. But over time, they developed the signature of the beaded patches.

You begin by drawing an image on canvas. Most Indians come up with an image they want to represent that year and find someone who has a pretty fair hand in drawing to sketch it out. Others draw their own. You want more details in the drawing to get a more significant patch.

Most of the time, the drawers are people behind the scene. It might be your niece or your neighbor down the block. The glory is in coming up with the design of the suit and the sewing—choosing the size, shape, and color of the beads, putting in the tedious man-hours of getting that patch beaded, and then building the suit.

Romeo Bougere, Big Chief of the Ninth Ward Hunters, in his 2006 suit. The Ninth Ward Hunters mask in with pictoral beadwork and ostrich plumes [*see "Passing on a Tribe," page 109, for more details on the Ninth Ward Hunters*]. Photograph by Debbie Flemming Caffrey.

Ostrich Plumes

Back in the 1950s and early 60s, uptown Indians made a conversion from turkey feathers on the crowns to ostrich plumes. Other Indians say Lawrence Fletcher, the Big Chief of the White Eagles, was the first one to wear them. From that time on, they grew to be associated with pictoral beadwork. The plumes make a very beautiful costume because the feathers flow with the movement of the body, and you can see the crown blocks away.

Years ago, the Lower Ninth Ward Indians, the Ninth Ward Flaming Arrow, and the Shoshone Warriors used to wear the big mummy crowns found downtown. They went through a transition to smaller, more flexible crowns, and started sewing pictoral beadwork with ostrich plumes, too.

Top: Big Chief Lil Walter Cook. *Bottom:* Lil Walter with Malcolm "Wildman Mackey" Williams [*left*] and two of his Queens in fluorescent blue on Mardi Gras day. Remembering the lead up to that year, Lil Walter says, "I wasn't supposed to mask, but Indian practice started up and I could hear the drums and started to think about a suit again. I was looking for a fluorescent blue for my plumes and the dye company didn't want to do it. I went to Illinois, found the right color in an old material store, and dyed the feathers myself. They ranged in color from fluorescent to royal blue, purple blue, and gray."

Upset at the results, Lil Walter talked with Ronald about what he should do. Ronald recalls, "I told him, 'You could have just one feather in your crown, and you'd still be the Big Chief of the Creole Wild West.'" Photographs by Ronald W. Lewis.

Lil Walter Cook
Big Chief of the Creole Wild West

The Creole Wild West is the oldest tribe on record. The tribe traces the history back to the early 1800s. Lil Walter Cook has maintained the integrity of the tribe, and his gang is one of the best of the pictoral beadwork culture. He's a naughty little fella, but he casts a big shadow out there on the street.

The gang leaves from Walter's mother, Ms. Sadie's, hairdressing salon near LaSalle and Jackson, and walks all over the city. I saw him once on Super Sunday and he was coming out of Basin Street from uptown and he always carried two, three, four Queens and plenty of children. As he's coming up the street, I'm hearing the chatter, "Oh, that's Lil Walter, that's Lil Walter." And as he turned off Basin onto Claiborne with those queens spread across the street, it was one of the most beautiful sights I've seen. He's just innovative like that.

I became one of his biggest fans and started documenting the Creole Wild West through my photos. I start going by his house to watch him work on costumes, and he allowed me to get involved in his work. They got some who are good at what they do, but they can't make changes. Then they got those who not only make a pretty suit, but create different images as they go along every so often. Lil Walter brought other influence into the Mardi Gras Indian suit by using lace as a trim on costumes. He also used "spotlight trim" that comes in silver and gold and has a diamond look. You usually see it on carnival ball regalia. In 2007, he created a whole new image by using buckskins.

03/18/20

Walter explains the evolution of his designs. *Left*: "For years I was using lace material over satin to make a brighter look on my suits." *Above*: "The year after Katrina, I took it to a different style—the Native American. My mom's people are Choctaw and she encouraged me to do it. I was concerned because I didn't want people to think I was mocking them.

"In the late 1990s, I went to a powwow in Albuquerque, the Gathering of the Nations, where more than 100,000 Indians from all over the world come together every year. When I was putting together the suit, I looked at pictures I took while I was there. I made the suit with brown buckskin with a chest plate made of bones, and used turkey quills and ostrich plumes to create a Mohawk look for my crown." Photographs by Norman Cook.

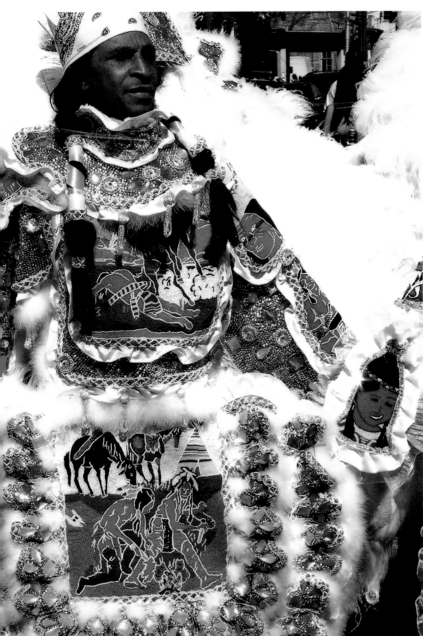

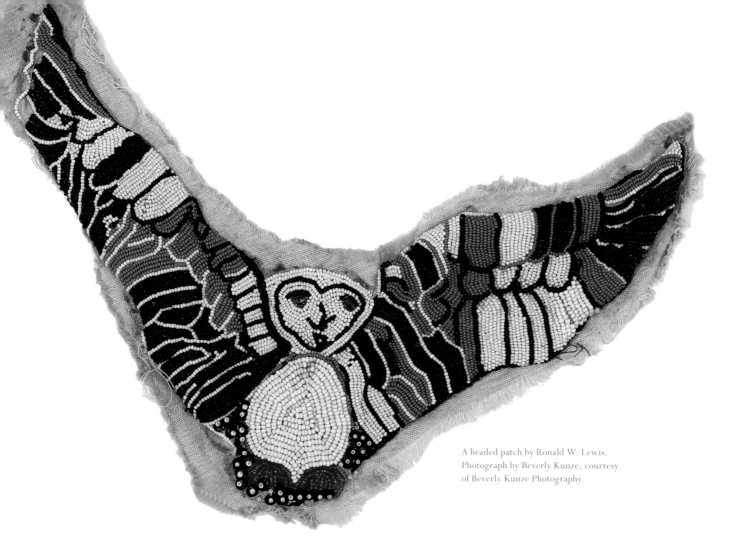

A beaded patch by Ronald W. Lewis. Photograph by Beverly Kunze, courtesy of Beverly Kunze Photography.

Surprise: Wings and Layers

Over the years, Indians who mask in the uptown style started layering suits to incorporate elements of surprise. Wings are attached to the trail of a crown and Indians put loops on them to hold them. Normally they keep them closed so you won't see what's on the front of their suit. When they open their wings, they're saying, "Now take that!"

Layering offers another layer of surprise: "If you think that's pretty, let me raise this up and show you what I got under there." Now some of them have something that just jump out at you and run you off, but you need to make sure the underwork is better than what's on top.

There is a fella who masked out of the Eighth Ward and he was meeting Big Chief Aaron "Booky" Freetime of the Ninth Ward Apaches at LaSalle and Washington on St. Joseph Night. He stood there with his wings closed. Booky was talking and talking about how he was prettier, and the fella didn't say nothing. But when he opened his wings, there was a real child standing in costume. Everybody was like, "WHAT?!" I told Booky, "Let's turn around. That was too much." Those are the type of the events that be etched into your mind about what they do with their costumes.

Big Chief Reginald "Suge" Williams. Photograph by Ronald W. Lewis.

Reginald "Suge" Williams
Big Chief of the Cheyenne Hunters

To make a good suit, Indians fill every available space. They don't want to leave no stone unturned. Reginald Williams, who we call Suge, and his brother Tony masked uptown off of Third and Rocheblave with the Golden Blades when they were young. In more modern times, Suge showed up as Big Chief of the Cheyenne Hunters in the Seventh Ward, but still masked in the uptown style.

When you look at his work, it's just exquisite. It's pictoral beadwork, but it looks like it has depth to it. He is one of the first to bring back an old style of masking—beading the headboard of his crown to create a picture instead of just using rhinestones. To show you how complicated an Indian suit can be, look at the beadwork of his "rabbit ears," which hang down from his crown, the "plat bands" that cover the hair from his wig, the "choker" around his neck, the "cuffs" on his wrists, and, of course, his wings.

Opposite page: Alphonse "Dowee" Robair, Gang Flag of the Red Hawk Hunters, donated one of his beaded patches to the museum. Dowee learned to sew from his father, Richard "Ivory" Turner, who is now the Second Chief of the Red Hawk Hunters. In this patch, Dowee depicts an Indian riding with the severed head of a white man. The remains of his body hang from a tree in the background. Light green arrows on the horse indicate that the scene is the aftermath of a battle. The letters on the horse, CTC, stand for "Cross the Canal," another name for the Lower Ninth Ward. Behind them is the name of the Robairs' Indian tribe, Red Hawk.

Top left: The family tradition of sewing pictoral beadwork continues as Dowee's wife, Trimika Robair, has joined the gang as Gang Squaw. The Robairs sew together and made a suit for their 11–month–old daughter, Peyton, in 2007. Photograph by Rachel Breunlin. *Right:* At the museum, candles decorated with photographs of Mardi Gras Indians, beads, feathers, and sequins include an image of Alphonse Robair. The candles were made by Ann Marie Coviello. They are on display in a shrine-like assemblage with stylized African figurines Ronald purchased at the Family Dollar. The beaded collars symbolize the beading traditions across the African diaspora. Photographs by Devin Meyers of Fotos for Humanity.

Flag donated by Darryl Preston on display at the House of Dance & Feathers. Photograph by Devin Meyers of Fotos for Humanity.

The Practice and the Street

Top: Ray "Hatchet" Blazio, Big Chief of the Wild Apaches, plays the tambourine at an Indian practice at the Tremé Music Hall. Hatchet had been going to Indian practice for more than 40 years. He remembers, "I lived on Annette Street in the Seventh Ward, and my uncle lived on 1828 Marais. Tootie Montana lived upstairs at 1827 ½ and held practice on the corner at a place called the Monogram Bar. When I was nine years old, I used to come around there on Sundays and Tootie would let a few of my friends and me come through the back door to show us a few things before running us off again.

"A lot of the fellas who worked for the company, driving the truck and delivering, used to hang at that bar. When Tootie decided to pull his own gang after masking with the Eighth Ward Hunters, he named the gang after this spot where he practiced. They became the Monogram Hunters. He kept that gang until the early 1960s, and then became Big Chief of the Yellow Pocahontas." Photograph courtesy of Sylvester Francis and the Backstreet Cultural Museum.

Bottom: Greg Sellers and Franklin "Wingy" Davis, who both masked with the YPH, at the the Tremé Music Hall, courtesy of Sylvester Francis and the Backstreet Cultural Museum. Wingy says, "I wanted to learn everything: Not only how to sew and make a suit, but how to dance, sing, and the meaning of different signals. I used to ride to practice with Thomas Sparks and Charles Taylor— we'd meet up with Jake Millon at his practice, then go to the Wild Magnolias, the Black Eagles. Every Sunday I'd get on the floor. The more you practice, the better you get at it. I was determined to do it right. I learned a lot of lyrics from Hatchet. I learned the basics and then the real me came out, singing about my own experiences. They teach you to be you—not just a carbon copy." Photograph courtesy of Sylvester Francis and the Backstreet Cultural Museum.

At practice, the tribes get together—they drum and sing and chant for hours—going through the ritual they would do on the street.

When you are sewing all the time to make it for Mardi Gras Day, Indian practice is one place you can count on to reconnect with your friends and get recharged. It's a party they give on Sunday at local bars. These little neighborhood spots become synonymous with the community; they are part of history and where the teaching happens. The Spyboy, the Flagboy, and everybody acclimates themselves to their positions and understands what their responsibilities are.

If you're having a practice, everybody's going to come to your practice. And when your practice is over, you go to the next person's practice. You get to know the people outside the costumes, you build relationships with them, and end up sharing old war stories at their local bar. When I was young, I used to be out to three and four o'clock in the morning on a Sunday and have to go to work a few hours later. That's how much fun it was. To go there and to get all pumped up and hyped, there's nothing else like it. It's an intense thing.

Once you hear the beat of the cowbells, drums and tambourines, and the chant of the people, it's infectious. I always say all good Indians have their

Big Chief Keith "Kiki" Gibson of the Comanche Hunters during Mardi Gras in 2003 on the corner of Charbonnet and Rocheblave in the Lower Ninth Ward. On Mardi Gras morning, Kiki explains, "All my Indians come around me while I'm trying to finish my suit and sing songs. Once I come outside, I start singing "Indian Red," our opening prayer, and call each one of my Indians before me to show off their suits. I used to be nervous, but now the adrenaline is flowing and I'm so excited to see my Indians and critique their suits. I call my Wildman first, then my Spyboy, my Flagboy, and my Gang Flag. Then I call my children—I usually have four or five mask with me—and my Big Queen. They get in a big circle around me, and I call myself. After I do my lil dance, I say 'counter fade,' which means to halt—to stop the prayer. Then I start up another song and we proceed down the street to meet different tribes. Every year, we're one of the prettiest gangs on the street." Photograph by Ronald W. Lewis.

own tambourine. It's like a journalist with typewriter. I'm attached to the traditional songs and rhythms. The Indian prayer is "Indian Red." It starts your day off and closes it. "Shoo Fly," "Shallow Water," and "Handa Wanda" are traditional songs. You think about "Shoo fly, don't bother me." Those words say: "Hey, get away from me" or "Sew, sew, sew all night long"—even the outsiders can listen to those songs and understand the meaning behind them. This next generation brought the hip-hop era into the culture. Now when they sing about "Fire in the hole," you know trouble is coming.

On Mardi Gras day, the Indians of a tribe meet at the Big Chief's house, and then walk through their neighborhood to the places where tribes are known to meet and go through the ritual battles of the Mardi Gras Indians. On Mardi Gras day, there are too many activities going on, so you make your choices. Sometime, if you can cheat a little bit and try to sneak uptown to LaSalle and Washington or

Derrick Magee as Wildman of the Wild Magnolias. Photograph by Ronald W. Lewis.

Second and Dryades before traffic gets too heavy and maybe catch an Indian or two before coming back downtown around Orleans and Claiborne to wait for the uptown tribes to make their way downtown. A lot of times the downtown ones go uptown to meet them on their own turf, too.

Walking through the neighborhoods gives the people that don't really come out for Mardi Gras an opportunity to be part of carnival. The senior citizens will come out on their porch and wave at the Indians. The children that won't travel those distances on Mardi Gras day will get a chance to see the costumes. I have a problem with the new generation of Mardi Gras Indians who would rather rent U-Hauls and not parade through the neighborhood. That takes away the story of masking because as you march on that journey, so many events go on before you get to your final destination. It's surrounding you.

Those events that happen out there on the streets in the process of marching into battle stay with you for years. The Wildman is the bodyguard of the tribe. He's not going to let anyone get close to the Chief. The Spyboy's responsibility is to seek out and pass on information to the chief that there's a tribe in the area. The Flagboy is the messenger for the Spyboy. He passes on the signals from the Spyboy to the Big Chief. And the Big Chief uses his staff to send a message back to let the tribe know if he's ready to meet another gang. Some times, he does certain things with his staff to let them know there is trouble in the area.

The Chief is a dictator. He's the big Kahuna of his tribe. I've seen some Flagboys and Spyboys and thought, "Well, that's a Big Chief's suit." It's happened before, but it don't mean nothing—that's the prettiest suit at your position. The Big Chief is just who he is: He's still the Big Chief. That's the difference. If he decides not to mask, he can determine who's going to bring the gang for that year. When he tell ya, "You need to go on your own," it's cause he has issues.

If you just pop up out of the clear blue sky and say, "I'm Big Chief," you'll have trouble on your hands. They ain't gonna respect you. They ain't gonna acknowledge you. Not in practice or nowhere else. It's how you present yourself out there on the streets, is how you is accepted. If you're out there and think that the Mardi Gras Indian world owes you something, that nobody's better than you, and

Darryl Preston, Spyboy of Red Hawk Hunters, in the Lower Ninth Ward in 2004. Photograph by Ronald W. Lewis.

Big Chief Tyrone Casby from Algiers. In the 1930s, his great uncle, Frank Casby, was the original Big Chief of the Mohawk Hunters. When he was 16 years old, Tryone began masking with the gang as Second Spyboy under Big Chief Raphael Parker. In 1980, he became the Big Chief. His own children have masked since they were four years old. Tyrone sews in both creative designs and pictoral beadwork. In 2004, his suit followed the downtown "monogram" style. His color scheme was chosen in honor of his son, who had just joined Mega Psi Phi Fraternity. Their colors are purple and gold. Photograph by Ronald W. Lewis.

you credit nobody for their work, they just overlook you. But if you come out as a Big Chief, and you've really paid dues into the system, they will acknowledge you.

From talking to the older Mardi Gras Indians, you would signify your manhood to be out there. Take someone like Chief Tyrone Casby. He's a principal in the New Orleans school system. His tribe, the Mohawk Hunters, is the only tribe that comes from the Westbank and their followers show up in force—crossing the Mississippi River in a school bus! You can hear them coming up the street from blocks away. They have all kinds of instruments: cowbells, airhorns, drums. Chief Casby is a great Mardi Gras Indian singer, too. He can carry a song for an extended period of time. It's all in the cadence of the song, and the chant and response of it. In the way he sings with his gang, you can tell he has control over the street.

Just like in the documentary, *All on a Mardi Gras Day*, when Royce Osborn says, "It's a warrior culture." These men were proud warriors, and when they got out there on that street, they showed all their proudness: "I'm Spyboy so and so." "Flagboy." "Big Chief." I always say, when you recognized by your peers for what you do, that's one of the greatest accolades that you can receive. People who are in the culture know that your commitment shows, when you show up, they know that, "Hey, he's committed to this thing."

I have a vast collection of photographs of Big Chiefs, but then I have photos of the other ones that play roles in the culture, too. It's not just the main players who make beautiful suits and I try to show appreciation for all these individuals. Those that wore them, and those who helped create them.

Opposite page: Renowned beader Joe Scott learned to sew from Felton Brown, the Second Chief of the White Eagles, when Felton came out of Angola, Louisiana's state penitentiary. Joe masked with the White Eagles as Gang Flag and then moved over to the Creole Wild West and ran Gang Flag for Lil Walter Cook. Since he stopped masking, he has sewn patches for countless Indians. He says, "When the suit is finished, you can't see a name on it, but they'll know. I'm color conscious. I know how much color to use." Scott's patches are recognizable for their tight beadwork and his use of gray, which can be seen on this canvas sewn for Big Chief Edgar Jacobs, of the Choctaw Hunters. Photograph by Rachel Breunlin.

Sewing Together

Left: Big Chief Gerald "Jake" Millon of the White Eagles. Photograph by Ronald W. Lewis. *Right:* Joe Pete Adams, who ran Flagboy for the White Eagles and became the Big Chief of the Seminoles. Photograph by J. Nash Porter.

Most Indians rely on a community of people to help them make it for carnival day.

The great Tootie Montana, for example, worked closely with his wife, Ms. Joyce, to make his legendary suits. But unless you are close to a gang, you probably won't know all the other people who contribute. It's just like a clothes designer in New York. That clothes designer puts out the design of the clothes, but it's his staff that helps him sew it. In the end, who does the credit go to? Does it go to seamstress that puts together the design? Usually, it goes to the designer.

For years, I sewed for Ricky Gettridge the YPH way—on cardboard. I masked a few little times, too, but I wasn't one of those renowned Mardi Gras Indians. I ended up liking to help out on a suit more than masking. When you're making a suit to wear,

it's so personal that you're consumed by it. But when you're helping somebody, you have the enjoyment of working with other people, and spreading your ideas around.

I knew of Edgar Jacobs out of the Seventh Ward. He paraded with Ricky when he was in the Bucket Men, drove a big old fancy Eldorado convertible, and always was a sharp dresser. In 1988, he moved into the Lower Ninth Ward on Garden and Urquhart Streets, and I'd run into him. He was masking as Spyboy with the Seminoles under Joe Pete Adams and David Beaulieu. The Seminoles were an Eighth Ward gang, but Joe Pete had masked uptown for years with the White Eagles, and the Seminoles masked in that

style. When Edgar moved to the Lower Nine, his style of sewing already fit into the scene.

I was interested in learning how to sew pictoral beadwork to know the best of both worlds. I asked Edgar to teach me how to do it. Once he put it on the rack, did that sewing, and then showed me how to tie down the beads, it became second nature.

In 1990, Edgar asked me if I wanted to mask again. I said, "Yeah, I'll do it one more time." A tribe can have as many as it wants at each position. The one with most seniority is the First Spyboy, but you might run two or three deep. Edgar was First Spyboy and I ran Second Spy.

Over time, Keithoe Jones became the Big Chief of the Seminoles and brought the gang to the Lower Ninth Ward. But by that time, we had already started another tribe.

Left: Big Chief Edgar Jacobs comes out of the newly formed Choctaw Hunters. Edgar reflects on preparing for the first year: "I was from the Seventh Ward and had never really been to the Lower Ninth Ward. My wife, Janice Jacobs, is from the neighborhood, and she brought me down there when we got married." Since he's been sewing a Big Chief's suit, Edgar's adopted brother and sisters, Agnes, Patricia, and Audy Anderson, have helped him. He says, "I didn't have any siblings and they took me as their own. They're like me, from the Seventh Ward and moved to the Lower Ninth Ward. They were with me from the beginning to help with sewing, money, and moral support." *Center:* Ricky Gettridge with Rashad Lewis and other members of the Choctaw Hunters. Ricky helped to sew Rashad's suit. *Right:* Coming back to the Lower Nine.

I had made Edgar an offer after we masked together. If he would become a Big Chief down in the Lower Ninth Ward, we would provide him with a gang. Soon after, I joined Peter Alexander, Big Troy Smoot, Ricky Gettridge, Edgar Taylor, and a number of other people at Peter's beauty salon to form a tribe.

The first year, we masked four little boys—my son Rashad, my nephew Brendt, Lil Rodey Track, Lil Richard Dunbar. And then other adult Indians came on board, and before long we were a full tribe. We named ourselves after a little street in the Lower Ninth Ward called Choctaw Alley between Flood Street and Andrews. It ended up giving our gang a Native American name as well.

When you look at the Polaroid picture of Edgar coming out his door, and the streets were lined with people to see the Big Chief of the Choctaw Hunters—that scene was second to none. We paraded around the Lower Nine and crossed the St. Claude bridge with people coming out of their community to follow our tribe into battle. We created a new cultural identity.

Second Chiefs

Troy Smoot was our Second Chief. He was Spyboy with Edgar with the Seminoles and became Second Chief of the Choctaw Hunters. He grew up in the Lower Nine, and was a cook. He was a big ol youngster with a lot of spirit, and when we formed the Choctaw Hunters, he was full of fire. He hired Joe Scott to design his first suit. Joe is one of the greatest sewers in the Mardi Gras Indian culture. He's like an artist with a needle. Very tight.

each other on Deslonde Street. He was the head custodian over NOCCA for years, and is a cosmetologist by trade.

In 1995, he was supposed to be his brother's best man at his wedding. It was close to Mardi Gras, and his wife was about to have a baby. When she went into labor the day before the wedding, I filled in as best man, and then went to his house

Left: Troy Smoot as Second Chief of the Choctaw Hunters. *Center:* Troy with his son, Troy Junior, who, as Little Chief, was dressed in green to match his godfather, Big Chief Edgar. *Right:* Peter Alexander in his powder blue suit on Mardi Gras Day. Photographs by Ronald W. Lewis.

When you saw Troy walk up the street, he had height and mass to him, and I said, "Look at Wide Body." I had affection for him because he brought a certain kind of excitement to our tribe. He got shot right there on Urquhart Street around 1995. We gathered ourselves together, other Mardi Gras Indians from around the nation came, and we gave him a traditional sendoff. Some wore their suits, some put a feather in their head, and we sang the prayer "Indian Red." After the prayer, we sang those songs of glory.

Our Second Chief after Wide Body was Peter Alexander. We grew up across the street from

and got all the pieces he was working on for his Indian suit. I called everybody I could think of and said, "I got all of Pete's stuff, he's already sewn the stones, we just got to put it together." We cut out his aprons and his jackets. We worked from that Sunday before Mardi Gras until Mardi Gras morning putting that suit together. Big Chief Rudy Bougere from the Ninth Ward Hunters, Gilbert "Cosmo" Dave, and all them came and helped. Peter had a beautiful daughter, and still made it on Mardi Gras day.

Shorty in three suits designed by Ronald. Photographs by Ronald W. Lewis.

Wildman

Our Wildman's name is Willard "Shorty" Walker. We've just been knowing each other for years. He decided he wanted to mask, and I told him I'd help him. The suit I made identified him with him being a warrior. Stature-wise, he's a small person, but he wore the suit big. And that is what gained his credibility out there in the society—for such as small person, he was such a fierce Wildman. Shorty's red suit was the award winning suit. For St. Joseph Day, the Mardi Gras Indians have a competition. When they call up the Wildmen to go up on stage, you want to put forth your best for the judges. And in the Wildman competition, he was top dog.

Top: Ronald with Rashad, masking as Spyboy for the Choctaw Hunters. *Bottom:* Aaron "Booky" Freetime [*right*] and Gilbert "Cosmo" Dave [*left*]. Photographs by Ronald W. Lewis. Ronald put together a "dream team" to help sew his son Rashad's Indian suits. He says, "It was me, Ricky Gettridge, Lil Walter Cook, and Cosmo—one of the greatest Indian sewers who never wore a suit." Cosmo's mother was a seamstress. He remembers, "When I was a little boy, my mama took me by the hand and showed me the Mardi Gras Indians. When I got older, I hooked up with the real boys.

"I enjoy creating the suits. There are people in the shadows that make Mardi Gras happen. That's how I look at myself. I love to go out on carnival day to see how people react to the suit—I love being behind it and representing it. Let's go get em! I got a needle and thread stuffed in my back pocket just in case something happens out there on the street. I'm prepared."

In 1993, the dream team sewed a yellow Spyboy suit for Rashad. The Choctaw Hunters carried a big second line. Ronald says, "The whole hood! Everybody who ever masked Indian or wanted to. We got a song we sing when we're going over the bridge, 'Ninth Ward, here we come!' It's like Hannibal crossing the mountain."

Cosmo joins in, "When we made it uptown, we met up with another gang that had a yellow Spyboy, too. I had sewed for him years ago. His second line started talking trash. One of them raised up his apron and said, 'You can't beat this!' Underneath was all beadwork I created more than ten years ago. It was still looking sharp. I jumped up and said, "You want to talk fire to us, who Spyboy you is?"

If they're gonna come at us with all that noise, I made them know it. I made him say it: 'I'm your Spyboy, Cosmo.'"

In the years that followed, Cosmo branched off to help start another gang, the Ninth Ward Apaches, with another member of the Choctaw Hunters, Aaron "Booky" Freetime. He says, "Booky was my glory."

Spyboy Darryl Preston of the Red Hawk Hunters wearing his crown with the acronym, "CTC" beaded onto the headboard. "CTC" stands for "Cross the Canal," another name for the Lower Ninth Ward. Photograph by Elliott Hammer.

Passing on a Tribe

Big Chief Rudy Bougere. For years, the Ninth Ward Hunters were known around the city of New Orleans, but when their Big Chief, Rudy Bougere, moved to California, the gang split up. Some members started masking with the Seminoles and the White Eagles, and others started the Ninth Ward Warriors under Big Chief Ira "Ralo" Rawlins. In 1984, Rudy came back home from California, and hoped to restart his tribe. Rudy went to his former Wildman, Richard "Ivory" Turner, who was now masking with the Warriors, and asked him to speak with Ralo about getting his tribe back. As it turned out, although Ralo was more than capable of building a Big Chief's suit, he preferred to have a different position. As Alphonse "Dowee" Robair, Ivory's son, explains, "As a Big Chief, you are more of a father figure to the other guys. You'll expect to get calls dealing with things other than Mardi Gras Indians." Ralo then masked as Second Chief of the Ninth Ward Hunters under Rudy's leadership. Photograph donated by Robert "Big Bob" Starks.

The passing down of a tribe isn't easy.

When a big chief retires, he has to think about all the people who invested their time and energy as members of his gang—family, friends who feel like family, and other supporters—and then decide who would be best to replace him.

Big Chief Rudy Bougere of the Ninth Ward Hunters was one of the more flamboyant chiefs. He was red with freckles in his face and cherries tattooed on his neck. And the way he sang! He was another one of them powerful singers that added a lot to the songs that didn't exist before. And that was Rudy. He was respected like that.

When he retired, he decided to give the gang to his Second Chief, Nelson Burke, but then changed his mind and made his son, Romeo Bougere, Big Chief. When you talk about how Romeo took the lead, and Nelson started his own tribe, you're talking about a story of the real brotherhood found in Mardi Gras Indian culture.

Big Chief Rudy passed away in November of 2003. This memorial is up at two of the main supply shops for Mardi Gras Indians, Jefferson Variety and Ms. Helen's Broadway Bound, and can be found on t-shirts and websites all over the country. Rudy's son, Romeo Bougere, remembers, "He was crazy. That dude would tell you anything. The doctor told him he couldn't put on a suit anymore. But he was hardheaded, and did it one more time before he passed on the tribe."

Nelson Burke was like an adopted son to Rudy. Born and raised in the Lower Ninth Ward, he ran Flagboy for the Ninth Ward Hunters for ten years before moving up to Gang Flag and then Second Chief. When Rudy realized he was going to have to retire, Nelson says, "He broke the feather and gave it to me. That's the symbol of passing on the tribe. It usually happens on St. Joseph Night or Mardi Gras evening, but this time it took place at a party. It's seen as the Chief's last time doing something with the tribe before he passes it on.

"There was a tribal meeting and Rudy asked everyone, 'Are you gonna be in front of Nelson? Accept his leadership?' And everyone said yes. But Rudy changed his mind, and gave the tribe to Romeo. The rest of the tribe left in protest, and we decided to form the Red Hawk Hunters.

"Before he died, Rudy tried to fix it. He offered the tribe again, but by that time we had decided to start Red Hawk. Once you say you are going to do something, you got to do it. Romeo's rebuilt the Ninth Ward Hunters and the gang is doing really well." Photograph donated by Romeo Bougere and his grandmother, Dorothy Hill.

A collage of photographs of Rudy Bougere, put together by his family for his funeral service. The small boy dressed as an Indian is Romeo, and in the bottom middle photograph on this page is Nelson Burke's red and white flag for his flagboy suit. Romeo says that before his father's death, "I was supposed to come out with a new tribe called the Young Generation. That year, just a few months before he passed, Nelson didn't mask and my father was mad. He told me since I had been sewing, I'd be Big Chief of the Ninth Ward Hunters instead. I was only 18 years old and I had some big shoes to fill. I masked as Big Chief that year, but after my father died, I supported Red Hawk Hunter the next two years. It was a hard position to be in. Nelson was like my father's other son. All my life I've known him, and he's an older brother to me. I still tell him to this day, I would love to run under him. I respect

saenger's Xmas par

"grandson Ge
"Toni"

him as my Big Chief, but once you become one yourself, you can't demote yourself. We talk about it all the time.

"I had to start over, and at first, no one respected me. No one believed in me and I had to develop a name for myself. During Indian practices, the other chiefs just saw me as this young, crazy ass dude and I'd get put out. They said they didn't want to meet me, but I kept coming back, and eventually, I started to gain their respect." Collage donated to the museum by Romeo Bougere and his grandmother, Dorothy Hill.

Romeo Bougere as Big Chief of the Ninth Ward Hunters in 2007. Romeo says, "You can't scream, 'I'm a Big Chief!' and not build a Big Chief's suit. After years of struggling, I really started sewing for Mardi Gras 2007. I made a stick and put heads on it of all the Indians that messed with me—the color of their scarves are the colors of their suits that year. I wanted to let them know, 'Don't play with me.'" Photograph by Ronald W. Lewis.

Dressed in purple, Nelson Burke shows off his comeback suit as Big Chief of the Red Hawk Hunters after Katrina in 2007. This year was the first time that Nelson and Romeo met on the street as Big Chiefs of two different tribes. Romeo says, "I was real anxious. I waited on the corner for him to come out for more than an hour. When we finally met, I was playing so hard, but he didn't meet me like he would meet another Big Chief." Nelson agrees, "He's right. I didn't meet him like I do the other cats. I didn't meet him as rough cause I look at him as a little brother." The moment was bittersweet. Romeo says, "We will always be family, but because we're two tribes, we don't collaborate. After we meet, he goes down the street one way, and I go the other." Photograph by Ronald W. Lewis.

Opposite page: Victor Harris, Big Chief of the Mandingo Warriors, Spirit of Fi Yi Yi. Victor explains how he chose the design: "This suit is the third coming of the beginning of Fi Yi Yi. It marked our 20th anniversary. Every ten years, I come back with the black suit and try to put the spirit of the previous nine suits into it. In 2004, I chose the four colors of Africa: Black is for the people, red is for the blood, green is for the land, and gold is for the richness of the land." Photograph by Jeffrey David Ehrenreich.

New Directions

Victor Harris as Flagboy of the Yellow Pocahontas. He's holding Cayetano "Tanio" Hingle, who has grown up to be the leader of the New Birth Brass Band. Photograph donated to the museum by Tanio Hingle.

Fi-Yi-Yi Vick 3-3-92

Victor Harris
Big Chief of Fi Yi Yi

Each generation of Mardi Gras Indians forms their own identity.

Outside the culture, the average person just sees a pretty costume, but if you spend time in the culture, over the years you learn about the stories that the costumes tell.

When you talk about Fi Yi Yi, they all are a tribe of their own—in their dress, in their character, and in how they present themselves on the street. That's what makes them so unique.

Victor started out with Tootie Montana as a Flagboy. He was really good. He always did make a good suit. In 1984, he started Fi Yi Yi. He said he had a premonition that it should be more African. From this premonition, he started designing his work off of African tribal designs with full facial masks.

It brought another level of social conciousness into the culture. Most people still mask as Indians. But in a lot of suits, you'll now see brown faces instead of red.

Victor Harris tells some of the origin story of Fi Yi Yi: "When I got put out of YPH in 1984, I asked the Lord why something like this could happen. I woke up one morning stretching and flexing and the words Fi Yi Yi started coming out of me.

"One year, a European visitor thought that the Mardi Gras Indians were real Native Americans. I understood how that could happen, but I thought, 'I'll never be mistaken again.' This is one of the reasons I started doing the African culture. I'm always thinking of my ancestors whenever I'm sitting at the table sewing. I always try and feel their spirit." Photographs by Ronald W. Lewis.

Red Hawk Hunters parading [*with Big Chief of the Seminoles Keithoe Jones behind them*]. Flagboy Terral Butler has sewn the continent of Africa on the front of his chest. He says, "My style of sewing is to show we're all one." Photograph by Debbie Flemming Caffrey.

Patches from Derrick Magee's biblical suit, worn in 2007, include scenes from Moses and the burning bush, the crucifixion, and Moses parting the waters. A lifelong resident of the Lower Ninth Ward, Derrick sewed the suit in honor of his community, "The biblical suit was for the Lower Ninth Ward. My grandmother and a couple other family members and neighbors passed away in the storm. It was a crisis and I wanted to dedicate the suit to my neighborhood. I grew up on 5432 Marais and everyone always liked to see me on Mardi Gras day. The white feathers represented clouds of joy." Photographs donated to the museum by Derrick Magee.

Some tribes have started telling their own histories and life stories within their costumes.[28]

The Seventh Ward Hard Heads are one of the tribes that are sewing beaded patches with new imagery. In 2007, the Big Chief of the Hard Heads, Otto DeJean, showed a lion and a Black man. Eddie "Big Easy" Vanison, the tribe's Gang Flag, had a large apron that said "Chocolate City," which referred to Mayor C. Ray Nagin's comment on Martin Luther King Day 2006 that New Orleans would remain a majority Black city after Katrina. That same year, Derrick Magee came out as the Big Chief of the Ninth Ward Navajo. He sewed a religious scene on his suit. It was big talk. Some didn't agree. They said, "That's not Indian," because it didn't have Indians on the patches. But after the storm, some of the younger generation want to tell about the changes that are going on in their lives.

Top: Photograph of Derrick Magee by Elliott Hammer. *Bottom:* Members of the Ninth Ward Navajo on Mardi Gras day near Shakespeare Park: Wildman Alonzo "Harry" Moore [*left*] and Gang Flag Terry Carr [*right*]. Terry explains why he decided to help form the Ninth Ward Navajo after after running Spyboy with Blackfoot Hunter, "I seen something in my Big Chief when he was masking as Wildman with the Wild Magnolias and the Young Cheyenne— –how he was building his suits—and I thought he needed to do something bigger than that. He needed to bring his own tribe. A lot of gangs are a whole lot of problems, but Derrick's about that thread and needle." For his first suit with Ninth Ward Navajo, Terry kept to a Native American motif. "I like to pick my own themes. I draw all my own stuff, too." Alonzo Moore's suit in 2006 was sewn with New Orleans in mind. He says it included "an Indian on the mountain top praying. It was a disaster year. It was a prayer for everyone to come back." Photographs of Harry and Terry donated by Derrick Magee.

Part IV

Social Aid and Pleasure Clubs

The Black Men of Labor Social Aid and Pleasure Club, according to co-founder Fred Johnson (former Spyboy for the Yellow Pocahontas), was "created to represent a different imagery of Black men than is often put out on the street. We are not pimps and gang bangers. We are working men who make a contribution to our communities." The club was started on the heels of a traditional jazz funeral for the legendary musician Danny Barker. Fred says, "That day, the music was so powerful, it was unbelievable. One the way back from the St. Louis Cemetery Number 1, the guys got to talking. The cats said, 'We really need to do this again.' Gregg Stafford from the Tuxedo Brass Band, Benny Jones from the Tremé Brass Band, and I got together and the first thing we decided was that our parade would hire traditional brass bands." Held on Labor Day weekend, their parade is, in part, inspired by the Longshoremen Union's Labor Day parades that used to occur in New Orleans. Photograph by Andy Levin.

The Young and True Friends Benevolent Association at a jazz funeral [*left*] and burying one of their members at the Green Street Cemetery [*right*]. Photographs by Jules Cahn, courtesy of the Historic New Orleans Collection.

"This [utopian] movement aims to defend and extend spaces for social autonomy . . . An immediate, non-negotiable politics is infused with a powerful sense of locality and a rootedness in tradition. 'It ain't where you're from,' intones Rakim, 'It's where you're at.'" — *Paul Gilroy*[1]

"Arrollar: rhythmic movement of a carnival dance group with people joining in behind, winding their way through the streets. It becomes a form of collective dance, marking time with the instruments of the congas and parades with a variety of agile steps and body movements, in circle formation, jumping, crouching and whirling, and improvising biting and erotic chants, while constantly on the move. The group of persons is so tightly packed that they roll along like a car and everything within its radius is swept up and carried along with the crowd." — *Rafael Brea and José Millet* [2]

INTRODUCTION

Social Aid and Pleasure Clubs

by Helen A. Regis

Contemporary African American social and pleasure clubs in New Orleans have a long tradition of autonomy that can be traced back to 19th century benevolent societies that provided health care and burial insurance for their members.[3] Widespread throughout the city, they functioned like insurance companies for their members, since most white-owned insurance companies at the time would not insure African Americans.[4] The organizations also hired physicians and pharmacists to provide health care for members and their families—and paid them a quarterly fee. Besides these tangible benefits, the clubs also encouraged thrift, fostered organizing and leadership skills, and provided a space for discussing the social issues of the day, as well as providing entertainment for their communities in the form of picnics, parades, dinners, and balls.

During the 1800s, at least some of these societies reached across social divides in the city. While some discriminated against potential members, other groups refused to operate on distinctions of class or caste. Claude Jacobs' research into the Girod Street Cemetery records shows that free blacks and slaves were being buried together in the same society tombs. Some groups, such as Dieu Nous Protège, worked to help slaves in New Orleans purchase their freedom, while others like the Artisans Society responded to the discriminatory membership requirements of other Creole organizations (which included certain levels of education, wealth, and knowledge of French) by keeping their membership open to all.[5]

By the 1860s and 70s, benevolent societies also began to play an important role as labor organizations. Some combined the functions of mutual aid and insurance with that of labor unions. The Longshoremen's Protective Union Benevolent Association (formed in April 1872) was like other benevolent societies, aiming "to relieve the distress of their members, care for the sick by providing physicians, nurses, and medicine, bury their dead and provide for their widows and orphans."[6] It differed, however, in one important respect as well: As a union, it proactively fought for the rights of workers along the waterfront. According to historian Eric Arnesen, the organizations demonstrated for the eight-hour work day "in the streets, meeting halls, and in the press...In March 1866, between 800 and 1,000 workers in numerous mechanics' and benevolent societies paraded in a 'grand procession' proudly displaying their banners down the city's main streets."[7]

In the 19th and early 20th centuries, women's clubs (called circles) were often affiliated with men's clubs, and they collaborated on impor-

The Young Men Olympian Junior Benevolent Association. Photograph by Ronald W. Lewis.

tant events, including anniversaries and other festivities. The Ladies Hope Aid Circle, for instance, served refreshments along the route of the Young Men's Hope Benevolent Association parade in 1887. Another women's group, the Vidalia Social and Aid Circle, was connected to the Young Men's Vidalia Benevolent Association and sponsored a fundraiser for the purchase of their society banner.[8]

Today, the Young Men Olympian Junior Benevolent Association is the only organization from that era still active today in the public celebration of anniversary parades, as well as the mutual aid and insurance functions. But as the narrative that follows clearly shows, many Social Aid and Pleasure Clubs active throughout the city trace their origins to the YMO.

Militias and Emancipation Celebrations

Parading traditions that contributed to what we know today as "second line" parades included

African processions and masquerades, Afro-Creole militias, Masonic ritual, and Irish, Italian, Spanish, and French Catholic saints' day processions. Prior to the Civil War, free people of color participated in militias, and these groups organized impressive parades and funerals for their members. The organization of people of African descent was a source of pride that could easily trigger fear and anxiety from the dominant social groups concerned about preserving their monopoly on political and economic power.[9]

In 1852, the abolitionist Frederick Douglass famously asked, "What, to the American slave, is your Fourth of July?"[10] and this question inspired a whole genre of alternative freedom marches and celebrations organized by African American communities throughout the United States. Many simply refused to observe a holiday that excluded them from the nation. These freedom celebrations were initially held in black churches and later developed into parades that challenged white authority and power. Historian Genevieve Fabre describes them as "a demonstration of orderliness and respectability on the part of those who claimed their right to be considered as fully responsible citizens."[11] As the celebrations took to the streets, military bands replaced the church choirs to become powerful counter ceremonies to mainstream Fourth of July events.

These processions commemorated outlaws and revolutionaries like Toussaint L'Ouverture and protested the Dred Scott decision. One participant, Jermaine Loguen, called for resistance and defiance of the 1850 Fugitive Slave Law: "I don't recognize this law—I don't fear it—I won't obey it! It outlaws me and I outlaw it."[12] After

the Civil War, associations, benevolent societies, and social clubs were part of a vast network of social groups that gave African Americans a place to analyze and strategize, to organize politically, and to be themselves. Organizations like the Grand Lodge and Knights of Reciprocity

On the other side of the Atlantic, a procession in Ghana, hosted by the Akuapem peoples in Akropong, seat of the paramount chief. Art historian Herbert "Skip" Cole explains, "Many festivals in Ghana are 'total works of art'...They commonly involve countless minor artistic forms and actions (i.e., songs, dances, sculptures, etc.) which can be seen as distinct, but whose separate nature is subsumed in such festivals by the impact of the whole, a continuous and unified event often of surpassing beauty and rich cultural significance."[14] Similar parades can be found throughout the African diaspora. Photograph courtesy of Herbert Cole.

sprang into action to protest the Democrats' segregation agenda with the 1890 Separate Car Act, and in their processions, they publicly displayed their presence and strength in numbers.[13] Contemporary parades in the streets of New Orleans have their own distinctive genealogies, traced to a collective memory of maroonage, defiance,

The CubaNOLA Arts Collective (founded in 1999 by Ariana Hall) has spent years exploring the cultural parallels between second line parades in New Orleans and conga parades in Santiago de Cuba, a city in Eastern Cuba that is culturally and historically linked to Haiti. In 2002, CubaNOLA spearheaded a cultural exchange between the Rebirth Brass Band, rooted in the New Orleans second line tradition, and La Conga de Los Hoyos, a marching organization in Santiago de Cuba, which was celebrating its 100th anniversary. During the 2002 carnival in Santiago, Rebirth and Los Hoyos marched down the streets together, traded musical instruments, and shared stories of their musical and parading traditions. *Left:* Los Hoyos in Santiago. Photograph by Helen Regis. *Right:* Derrick "Kabukey" Shezbie of the Rebirth Brass Band, playing in a Conga parade in Cuba. Photograph by Jacques Morial.

and freedom claimed from within an inequitable society. As Ronald put it,

> People have a lot of struggles in life. They cope and deal with it. We are strong people that have dealt with adversity from the time our ancestors hit the shores of the United States until now.

Caribbean Connections: Rara, Congas and Cabildos

Throughout West and Central Africa, stately ceremonial processions and dynamic spirit-filled masquerade dances express political and spiritual powers for all to see. In Haiti, Cuba, and elsewhere in the Caribbean, processions organized by Black social organizations bear close resemblance to New Orleans second line parades.[15] They engulf the streets of their cities, they draw people together, and they use music and dancing to create and express pride, joy, and solidarity. All of these Caribbean parades have African roots, but they are always changing, reflecting

the issues people are facing in their lives and expressing the creativity of the people. In Haiti, the parades are known as Rara. In Cuba, they are called Cabildos, Comparsas, and Congas.

Like second line parades in New Orleans, the Conga parades of Santiago de Cuba are the most public events for groups that function year round as social organizations. As CubaNOLA writes, "The Congas are bands and neighborhood social clubs that lead massive parades wherein the community takes center stage."[16] They move through diverse neighborhoods of the city, and express their creativity through costumes, music, and their distinctive parade themes. Like social club parades, which contributed to the development of early jazz, Santiago's Conga parades fostered distinctive rhythms that have shaped Cuban musical history. Both traditions have influenced popular music around the world.

In Haiti, Rara parades provide a striking analogy to New Orleans' second line with its insistence

Left: A Rara parade in Haiti, courtesy of Chantal Regnault. *Right:* Rara walks in the Artibonite Valley. Known as "popular armies," Raras, dressed in elaborate costumes, dance and play music that conveys religious, social, and political messages. Photograph courtesy of Elizabeth McAlister.

Politics & the Right to the City

Parading in public almost always has a political meaning—even when the clubs organizing the parades are mostly "social." After Katrina, the social club parades became more important than ever as they called people home to reclaim the city and say, "We are New Orleans," and "This is our city." And when so many residents were dealing with loss (of family members, friends, neighbors, as well as homes, material possessions, family photo albums, and personal archives), the parades—with their powerful ways of expressing grief and faith in collective perseverance and triumph over adversity—became important spaces for coming together and reflecting on life and community. When city officials tripled parade fees in the spring of 2006, the ACLU and the New Orleans Social Aid and Pleasure Club Task Force came together and sued on constitutional grounds. The city was forced to settle with the clubs when a federal court judge agreed with their case: Parading is constitutionally protected speech.

Second lines create a safe space for people from all walks of life to experience a moving festival of music, food, dance, and song. For people like me, who came to New Orleans from suburban places, the second line is a teacher as well—

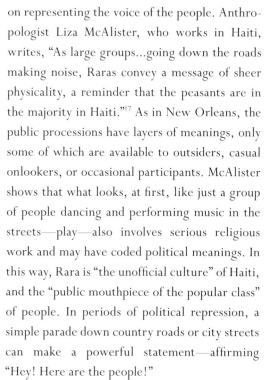

on representing the voice of the people. Anthropologist Liza McAlister, who works in Haiti, writes, "As large groups...going down the roads making noise, Raras convey a message of sheer physicality, a reminder that the peasants are in the majority in Haiti."[17] As in New Orleans, the public processions have layers of meanings, only some of which are available to outsiders, casual onlookers, or occasional participants. McAlister shows that what looks, at first, like just a group of people dancing and performing music in the streets—play—also involves serious religious work and may have coded political meanings. In this way, Rara is "the unofficial culture" of Haiti, and the "public mouthpiece of the popular class" of people. In periods of political repression, a simple parade down country roads or city streets can make a powerful statement—affirming "Hey! Here are the people!"

about how to be together in shared spaces in the city. We can dance together, rubbing shoulders alongside the band in the heat of the action, or we can walk on the edges of the parade at a more leisurely pace, catching up in conversations with old friends and meeting new ones. Music lifts us out of our worries and eases our fatigue, while dancing soothes our woes, and the solidarity across the crowd creates shared experiences. In the positive atmosphere of peoplehood created by the parades, we can imagine a future together. After the flood, my first second line parades back in the city with the Prince of Wales, Lady Buck Jumpers, and Big Nine gave me hope that we could rebuild our damaged city and make it whole for all its citizens.

What's ahead

This section of the catalogue maps out the contemporary social club scene from the perspective of Ronald and the Lower Ninth Ward. It is enhanced by the contributions of many social clubs and second liners from all over the city who have donated photographs and regalia to the House of Dance & Feathers, or are represented in images. Ronald's narrative and the long photo captions together tell the story of social clubs and second line parades in the recent history of New Orleans. We learn how the clubs function as community-based organizations and how participants honor their loved ones and remember those who have passed on through parade rituals that combine joyful celebration with sacred dirges and memorials. The names of the clubs and the meaning of the parades have changed since the days of reconstruction. But they continue to bring people together to express key values of respect, dignity, solidarity, honor, and style through coordinating parades, dance, and collective ritual of moving through the city together. And through the creativity of footwork and color-work, ritual play and design regalia, club members continue to express their individual and collective identities, and to reflect on what it means to be Black and to live in this America.

Left: Ricky Gettridge and Charlotte "Minnie" Lewis standing in front of the Katrina memorial in the Lower Ninth Ward at the Big Nine Social & Pleasure Club's second line in December 2006. *Right:* Members of the Big Nine parade passed National Guard soldiers in town after Katrina. The parade began in the Lower Ninth Ward and made its way across the St. Claude Bridge to Sweet Lorraine's, where the Black Men of Labor hosted a stop for them. Ronald recalls, "When we paraded in 2006 after Katrina, it had an emotional impact on people. Our community was being written off, and we stood up as an organization and said, 'We gonna show the world that we still exist. We're not going to accept people saying that we can't function as a people in the Lower Ninth Ward anymore.'" Photographs by Andy Levin.

Opposite page: The First Division of the Young Men Olympian Benevolent Association at their parade in 2007. The president, Alfred "Bucket" Carter, explains, "We have six divisions and ours is the one that keeps everything traditional." Organized in 1884, the YMO's annual second line takes place uptown every year on the fourth Sunday of September. Many men who began parading with the YMO have gone on to start their own social and pleasure clubs. Bucket says, "A bunch of them came from us. We're their mentors. They know how it goes, so they decide to try it out on their own. Some are a success and some not. Some come back and some keep going." Photograph donated by Alfred "Bucket" Carter.

Community—Based Organizations

Each year, social aid and pleasure clubs celebrate the anniversary of their organization with a second line parade.

All clubs are representatives of their communities, and your parade represents that. When you form a route, you are bringing people through the cracks and crevices of your neighborhood to give everybody an opportunity to be part of it. The parade has its political impact, as well as its social impact. We truly belong to the city.

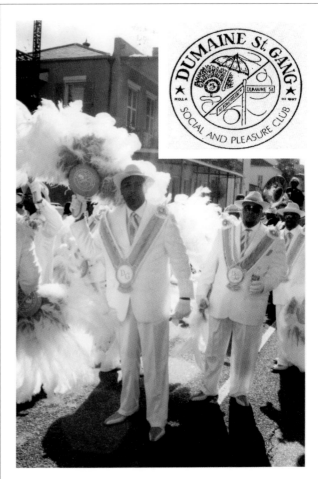

Top: Dumaine Street Gang Social and Pleasure Club's logo was designed by Charles Brazil. The logo, featured here from their 2004 route sheet, includes second line regalia and the street signs for N. Robertson and Dumaine Streets in Tremé, where the club originated. Many of the members used to gather at a corner store at this intersection to laugh and clown around. *Bottom:* President of the Dumaine Gang Byron Hogans, wearing antique gold and ivory, holds a fan with the club's logo on it during their parade. Photograph donated by Byron Hogans.

The Original Big Seven Social and Pleasure Club, based in the Seventh Ward, traces its roots back to the St. Bernard Public Housing Development, where many of the members were born and raised. In May of 2006, less than a year after Katrina, they came out of a gutted house across the street from the development, which remained closed with a chain linked fence around the perimeter. Despite protests, it was torn down in 2008. Photograph by Rachel Breunlin.

Robert "Big Bob" Starks, the business manager of the Big Nine Social & Pleasure Club, joined the club after being a sergeant in the army. He says, "They asked me to keep order and handle the club's business. I wanted to show off the Lower Ninth Ward. I used the discipline from the army to show them it can be done." In this photograph, taken at the 2004 parade, Big Bob shows off the "9" he commissioned Rudy Bougere, Jr., son of Big Chief Rudy of the the Ninth Ward Hunters, to make. Rudy used half–inch plyboard to make the design, and accented it with rhinestones "to sparkle in the sun like diamonds and gold." The colors—black, white, and gold—matched the colors of the First Division's suits (chosen in honor of New Orleans' football team, the Saints). It was the only thing still hanging on the wall of his house after Hurricane Katrina. Photograph by Andy Levin.

Parading in the Lower Ninth Ward

To run a successful social and pleasure club, you have to have durability, and you have to be good at decision and policymaking. One of the most original clubs that came out of the Ninth Ward area was the Ninth Ward Rulers. And from the Ninth Ward Rulers out came the original Double Nine Social and Pleasure Club, but those were organizations that didn't sustain.[18] We formed the Big Nine Social & Pleasure Club with many of the members of the Choctaw Mardi Gras Indian tribe—Ricky Gettridge, Peter Alexander, and Big Chief Edgar Jacobs, along with Robert Starks, Melvin Davis and Kenny Turner, Kenny Dupont and Walter Ramsey. We were such a creative group of people that the parade became that other outlet to burn off some of that energy.

When a person says "the Tremé," they are evoking a history of cultural identity in New Orleans. For the Lower Ninth Ward, we were just known as the Ninth Ward, as fearless people. We didn't have cultural identity, and it feels good to have that now—through social and pleasure clubs like the Big Nine, the CTC, and Nine Times, and also our Indian gangs. To me, that is very important.

Many people have lived in this city and never crossed the St. Claude and N. Claiborne bridges over the Industrial Canal into the Lower Ninth Ward. People feared coming down here. The Central Business District people will say, "Don't go in the Ninth Ward." They had their own image of how this community looked and it was similar to images we saw during Katrina: They portrayed the Ninth Ward people as illiterate, poor, nonfunctional, and violent. They didn't have a legitimate reason for thinking so because they were in unchartered waters. When social and pleasure clubs began in our neighborhood, they brought hundreds and hundreds of people to this community to see parading in the Ninth Ward. People came down here and saw that we had nice big old wide streets and well tended houses, and that gave them a comfort zone. They saw that "Hey, this ain't what I thought it was."

A Big Nine parade rolls through the Lower Ninth Ward. Photograph donated by Robert "Big Bob" Starks.

Opposite page: Monique Jordan, the Queen of the CTC (Cross the Canal) Steppers, a social and pleasure club from the Lower Ninth Ward, honored her mother, Henrietta Kincey Jordan, who everyone knew as Happy, on the collar of her gown for the 2008 parade. Growing up back-a-town with her mom, Monique remembers, "There was never a dull moment. She worked at the voter polls, picked up money to help with funerals, gave barbeques in the neighborhood, and worked at Dunbar Elementary. She loved to party and hung out at the Welcome Inn, just a few blocks from our house. In the early 90s, she was a member of the Lower Ninth Ward's Double Nine and always wanted to be Queen."

The house on Alabo was destroyed in the flood, and the Jordan family relocated to Baton Rouge. Happy died in a house fire before she had the chance to reign as Queen. Monique says, "It's hard to get that position—it's like being Miss America for your community. When my turn came up in 2008, I did it in remembrance of her. I put the picture of her on my collar. We rode through our neighborhood and all my friends and neighbors were yelling, 'Go Monique! Do it for your mom!' Other people told me they were sorry, they didn't know she had passed." Monique donated the collar to the museum after the parade to preserve the memory of her mom's life in the Lower Ninth Ward. Photograph by Rachel Breunlin.

Honoring Relationships

Original Prince of Wales S&P
67 th Anniversary Parade

Introducing

The Lady
Wales

Sunday
September 10
1.00 P.M.
3801
Tchoupitoulas

Start: Rock Bottom Lounge 3801 Tchoupitoulas and Peniston. Back Peniston to Magazine St. Down Magazine to Louisiana Avenue. Left on Louisiana. Back Louisiana to Sandpiper Lounge. Stop!

Back Louisiana to Freret. Left on Freret to General Taylor. Right on General Tayor to Magnolia. Right on Magnolia to Silky's Lounge. Stop!

Down Magnolia to 2820 Magnolia to Shirley's "Place to Be". Stop

Down Magnolia to Washington Avenue. Right on Washington Avenue. Out Washington to Lasalle,left on Lasalle to Kemp's Lounge. Stop!

Down LaSalle to Third Street. Left on Third and out Third Street to Dryades to Charley Wright's Watering Hole. Stop!

Out Third to St. Charles. Right on St Charles; up St. Charles to Washington Avenue. Left on Washington Avenue. Out Washington Avenue to St. Thomas. Right on St. Thomas. Out St Thomas to Ma Mary's Watering Hole. Stop!

Up St. Thomas to Seventh Street- Juicy's Lounge. Stop!

Back Seventh Street to Annunciation. Left on Annunciation. Up Annunciation to Peniston. Left on Peniston. Out Peniston to Tchoupitoulas to Rock Bottom Lounge. Disband

1928

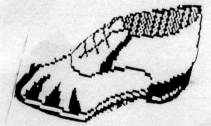

1995

Leave your guns and attitudes at home!!!

Routes

Second line season runs nearly every Sunday from late August to early May.

Most organizations have paraded on the same date for years. Clubs advertise their parade by creating route sheets that tells the date, time, and beginning location of their parade, and where it will be going. They pass them out in the weeks leading up to their day at other parades, neighborhood barrooms, and these days over the internet, to let people know where to find it. I've been collecting route sheets for years, and each one is different. You can learn a lot about a club by how they present themselves on paper.

Clubs usually start at a barroom or another community spot—it could also be somebody's house. Throughout the parade, they stop at different places to rest and show respect. When a bar gets put on a parade, it brings an economic windfall for that business. People are going to gather before we get there, buy drinks during the stop, and then many will stay after the parade passes.

Asking another club to host a stop for your parade is a way of showing respect for individual clubs in your community. It's like a communication thing.

Above: Dorn "Pappy" Kemp in front of his famous barroom. Photograph by L.J. Goldstein.

Opposite page: The Original Prince of Wales' 1995 route sheet, designed by Joe Stern, includes a stop at Kemp's. Joe recalls the role of the barroom in the uptown parade scene: "L.J.'s photograph brings back lots of memories— most of them happy. That's how I remember Pappy, standing on the chair by the door holding a Bud Light, and watching the members come in. There was a time, in the 1990s and early into 2000s, when almost every uptown parade stopped at Kemp's. It was a wondrous thing, all those throngs of people jumping to the music and then just hanging around socializing.

"Every Thursday night, Rebirth Brass Band played and the place was so crowded you could hardly get in. Sometimes the set didn't start until midnight and often ended by parading around the block. And no one ever complained. On Sunday night, from late September until Mardi Gras, Big Chief Peppy and the Golden Arrows had Indian practice back when children were allowed in the barroom just for that. Indians from all over (Larry Bannock, the Comanche Hunters, the Creole Wild West, and others) would come. A week or two before Carnival, you had it jammed full of people from all over the world, natives returned home and white folks from everywhere.

"It's funny, other than a party, these events were the only time Pappy ever had a crowd. Most days, the bar opened up during the day where a small steady crowd drifted in and out. For a long time they sold plate lunches— soul food like white beans and turkey necks—and were closed by nine P.M."

SUDAN

WHEN : NOVEMBER 12, 1995

WHERE : ST. BERNARD AVE. AND ST. CLAUDE AVE.

TIME: 1:00 PM.

PARADE ROUTE

START: KERLEREC ST. AND ST. CLAUDE AVE. TO ST. BERNARD AVE. .(TURN
LEFT ON ST. BERNARD AVE.) ST. BERNARD AVE. TO N. VILLERE ST. (RIGHT
ON N. VILLERE ST.) CONTINUE ON VILLERE ST. TO ST. ANTHONY ST.
(RIGHT ON ST. ANTHONY ST.) STOP IN THE MIDDLE OF THE BLOCK. CONTINUE
ON ST. ANTHONY ST. TO N. RAMPART ST. (RIGHT ON N. RAMPART) N. RAMPAR
TO URUSLINE ST. (RIGHT ON URUSLINE ST.) STOP AT 1232 URUSLINES ST.
CONTINUE ON URUSLINES ST. TO N. ROBERTSON ST. STOP AT TREME MUSIC HAL
(LEFT ON N. ROBERTSON ST.) N. ROBERTSON TO ORLEANS AVE. (RIGHT ON
ORLEANS AVE.) CONTINUE ON ORLEANS AVE. TO N. ROCHEBLAVE ST. STOP
GOLDEN TRUMPETS CONTINUE ON ORLEANS TO N. BROAD (RIGHT ON N. BROAD ST
N. BROAD TO ESPLANADE AVE. (RIGHT ON ESPLANADE AVE.) TO N. TONTI ST.
(RIGHT ON N.TONTI ST.) TO BARRACK ST.) STOP CONTINUE ON TONTI TO
URSULINES ST. (RIGHT ON URSULINES ST.) STOP IN MIDDLE OF BLOCK.
CONTINUE ON URSULINES TO N. DORGENOIS TO (LEFT ON N.DORGENOIS ST.)
N.DORGENOIS TO ST. PHILLIP ST.(LEFT ON ST. PHILLIP ST.) CONTINUE ON
ST.PHILLIP ST. TO N. CLAIBORNE AVE. STOP MONEY WASTER. CONTINUE ON
ST.PHILLIP (LEFT ON CLAIBORNE AVE.) CONTINUE ON N. CLABORNE TO ST.
BERNARD AVE. MAKE A RIGHT ON ST. BERNARD AVE. TO   LUCK STAR'S BAR
                    PARADE DISBAND !!!!!!!!

SUDAN SOCIAL AND PLEASURE CLUB ASK THAT YOU HELP US HONOR THE MEMORY
OUR DECEASED BROTHERS ARCHIE CHAPMAN, ROGER LEWIS, TAJU SMITH BANNERM
GILBERT AND MONEY WASTER "DUTE"

Opposite page: Sudan makes specific reference to their connections to Africa with their name, their regalia, and if you look closely on their 1995 route sheet, hand–drawn pictures of the continent. This route began in the Seventh Ward and went into the Sixth Ward. They are welcomed into this community by the Money Wasters Social & Pleasure Club on N. Claiborne at St. Philip. *Above:* Photograph of Sudan parading in November of 1992. Adrian "Coach Teedy" Gaddies, co-founder of Sudan, says, "It's a spirit. Our parade is for our community. It's not a fashion statement for us—it's about the celebration of the music. The beat of the drum. When that music starts, it ain't nothin nice." Photograph donated by Kenneth "Dice" Dykes.

MONEY WASTERS SOCIAL AID & PLEASURE CLUB
1998 ANNUAL PARADE

"COME KNOCK WITH US...KNOCK WITH US"

DATE: November 1,1998
FORMATION: 12:00 p.m.
STARTING TIME: 1:00 p.m.

QUEEN: DENISE SLATTER   KING: BRYSON CRAWFORD

START: **MONEY WASTERS CLUB HOUSE** AND **CALDONIA 2000**
ST. PHILIP& N. ROBERTSON ST. UP N. ROBERTSON TO N. VILLERE
ST. RIGHT ON N. VILLERE TO BASIN ST; RIGHT ON BASIN TO N.
CLAIBORNE AVE; LEFT UP N.CLAIBORNE TO BIENVILLE AVE.
RIGHT UP BIENVILLE TO N.DERBIGNY ST. STOP **D&D BAR,**
CONTINUE UP BIENVILLE TO N. BROAD ST. RIGHT ON N.BROAD
TO ST. ANN ST. STOP **ZULU CLUB,** CONTINUE DOWN N. BROAD
TO URSULINE ST. RIGHT ON URSULINE TO N. CLAIBORNE AVE.
LEFT DOWN N. CLAIBORNE TO GOV. NICHOLLS. RIGHT ON GOV.
NICHOLLS TO VILLERE ST. STOP **AFRICAN AMERICAN
MUSEUM.**CONTINUE OUT GOV. NICHOLLS TO TREME ST. STOP
CALENDER GIRLS. LEFT DOWN TREME TO BARRACKS ST.
RIGHT ON BARRACKS STOP **LIL PEOPLE'S.** CONTINUE OUT
BARRACKS TO N. RAMPART ST. LEFT ON RAMPART, DOWN
RAMPART TO ST. CLAUDE U- TURN ST. CLAUDE TO TOURO ST.
STOP **LORAIN'S DUGOUT.** UP ST. CLAUDE TO ST. BERNARD,
RIGHT ON ST. BERNARD TO N. ROBERTSON STOP **SUDAN.** LEFT
ON N. ROBERTSON ST. STOP **MONEY WASTERS KIDS.** UP N.
ROBERTSON TO LAHARPE ST. RIGHT ON LAHARPE ST. TO N.
CLAIBORNE AVE. LEFT UP N. CLAIBORNE AVE. TO ST. PHILIP ST.
LEFT ON ST. PHILIP ST. TO N. ROBERTSON DISBAND. 1st DIV.
CANDLE LIGHT AND 2nd DIV CALDONIA 2000

PLEASE LEAVE ALL YOUR PROBLEMS AT HOME AND ENJOY YOURSELF

LOVE, PEACE, AND UNITY

Above: Money Wasters parade on N. Claiborne. Their original headquarters was in the Sixth Ward on Orleans Avenue between N. Galvez and N. Johnson. Lois Andrews, a member of the Lady Money Wasters, says, "Every first Sunday of November, everybody was looking forward to going to our parade." *Opposite page:* In 1999, the Money Wasters' second line goes through the downtown neighborhoods of New Orleans. Sudan hosts a stop for them in the Seventh Ward. Besides hosting stops, clubs correspond in other ways to help support the year's parade season. Lois explains: "When another club has a function, other clubs get together to support them by buying raffle and dance tickets, going to picnics. They send correspondence letters to other clubs to let them know that they want to be sponsored. Say you have 12 members, you let them know that you are sending 12 tickets for them, and the club is responsible for the tickets." Photograph by L.J. Goldstein.

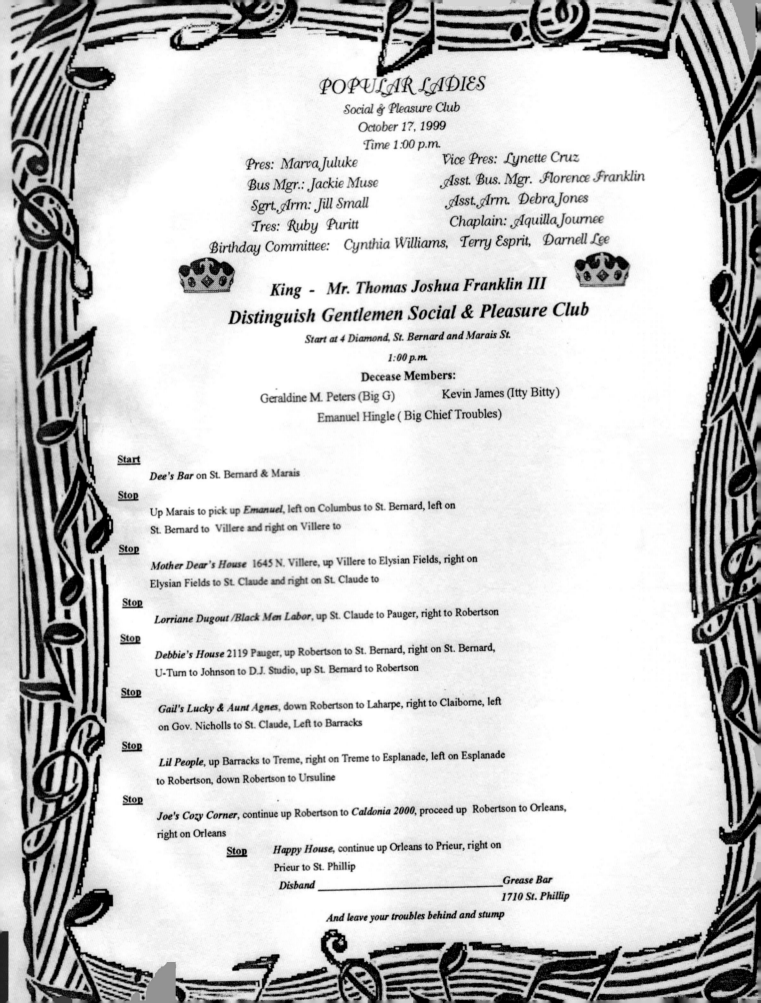

POPULAR LADIES
Social & Pleasure Club
October 17, 1999
Time 1:00 p.m.

Pres: *Marva Juluke*   Vice Pres: *Lynette Cruz*

Bus Mgr.: *Jackie Muse*   Asst. Bus. Mgr. *Florence Franklin*

Sgrt. Arm: *Jill Small*   Asst. Arm. *Debra Jones*

Tres: *Ruby Puritt*   Chaplain: *Aquilla Journee*

Birthday Committee: *Cynthia Williams, Terry Esprit, Darnell Lee*

King - Mr. Thomas Joshua Franklin III
Distinguish Gentlemen Social & Pleasure Club
Start at 4 Diamond, St. Bernard and Marais St.
1:00 p.m.

Decease Members:

Geraldine M. Peters (Big G)   Kevin James (Itty Bitty)

Emanuel Hingle (Big Chief Troubles)

Start   *Dee's Bar* on St. Bernard & Marais

Stop   Up Marais to pick up *Emanuel*, left on Columbus to St. Bernard, left on
St. Bernard to Villere and right on Villere to

Stop   *Mother Dear's House* 1645 N. Villere, up Villere to Elysian Fields, right on
Elysian Fields to St. Claude and right on St. Claude to

Stop   *Lorriane Dugout /Black Men Labor*, up St. Claude to Pauger, right to Robertson

Stop   *Debbie's House* 2119 Pauger, up Robertson to St. Bernard, right on St. Bernard,
U-Turn to Johnson to D.J. Studio, up St. Bernard to Robertson

Stop   *Gail's Lucky & Aunt Agnes*, down Robertson to Laharpe, right to Claiborne, left
on Gov. Nicholls to St. Claude, Left to Barracks

Stop   *Lil People*, up Barracks to Treme, right on Treme to Esplanade, left on Esplanade
to Robertson, down Robertson to Ursuline

Stop   *Joe's Cozy Corner*, continue up Robertson to *Caldonia 2000*, proceed up Robertson to Orleans,
right on Orleans

Stop   *Happy House*, continue up Orleans to Prieur, right on
Prieur to St. Phillip

Disband _____ **Grease Bar**

                                              1710 St. Phillip

And leave your troubles behind and stump

Memorials

When you look at New Orleans, this city is where people celebrate people's lives through the jazz funerals.[19] This was people's way of letting others know that person was special. In addition, many clubs will honor deceased members in their annual parades.

Opposite page: The Popular Ladies' second line in 1999 honored three deceased members: Geraldine M.Peters, Kevin James, and the Big Chief of the Trouble Nation Mardi Gras Indian Tribe, Emmanuel Hingle. Their first stop was also in honor of him. Aquilla Journee, a member of the Popular Ladies, explained, "Emmanuel Hingle always said he wanted to be our king, but that year didn't come up before he drowned. His family was living on Marais in the Seventh Ward. We come off the barroom on St. Bernard to their house, did a second line step, bowed, and said a little prayer." *Above:* Aquilla holds a fan she's saved from the Popular Ladies' parade in honor of Emmanuel. One side shows him dressed in his Mardi Gras Indian suit, and the other in a second line parade. Photographs by Rachel Breunlin.

BIG NINE SOCIAL AND PLEASURE CLUB
ALONG WITH
ANNIE MAE HIGH STEPPERS
AND
THE UNDEFEATED DIVAS

Sunday, December 19, 2004
Start Time: 12:00 Sharp

Queens for 2004
Mrs. Annette Denson & Ms. Deidra Howard

Kings for 2004
Mr. M.C. Action Jackson & D.J. Ro

Lady Ambassador
Mrs. Ethel Wicker

Big Shot
Mr. Henry Faggen

Grand Marshall
Mrs. Jean Morris

Honorary Grand Marshall
Mrs. Cherice Harrison - Nelson

Princess
Ms. Shatarra Ohillia

PARADE ROUTE

PARADE STARTS: 2530 Alabo Street (Phipps Inn) and continue to Florida Avenue (Stop) Exotic Soul Inn. Right turn on Florida Avenue, continue to Tupelo Street. Make right turn on Tupelo Street (Stop) 2600 Tupelo Street (Irvin's Restaurant and Bar). Continue down Tupelo Street to North Claiborne Avenue. Make right turn on North Claiborne Avenue and continue to Reynes Street and make a U-turn at Reynes Street heading back towards Tupelo Street. Make a right turn on Tupelo Street (Stop) 1300 Tupelo Street. Make left turn on Urquhart Street to Delery Street. Turn right on Delery Street and continue to St. Claude Avenue. Make right turn on St. Claude Avenue (Stop) 6311 St. Claude Avenue (Nell's Sports Bar). Continue up St. Claude Street (Stop) 5000 St. Claude Avenue (Mor's Lounge) (Disband)

DEDICATIONS TO OUR LOVED ONES WHO ARE GONE, BUT NOT FORGOTTEN:
Ms. Kim Groves
Mr. Edward (Red) Waterhouse, Sr.
Mr. Joseph Williams b-k-a Shot Gun
Mrs. Marion Wright

PLEASE LEAVE YOUR GUNS AND ATTITUDES AT HOME ! ! ! ! ! ! ! !

Opposite page: The Big Nine Social & Pleasure Club's 2004 route sheet honors members of their community ranging from Desire Public Housing Development community organizer Henry Faggen to the founder of the Mardi Gras Indian Hall of Fame, Cherice Harrison-Nelson. It also recognizes deceased members of the community, including Kim Groves and Joseph "Shotgun Joe" Williams, who were killed by New Orleans police officers in separate incidents. *Above left:* A drawing of Kim Groves reaching out over New Orleans that was on display at the Big Nine parade. Photograph donated by Robert "Big Bob" Starks. *Above right:* A photocopy of a drawing of Joseph "Shotgun" Williams, one of hundreds passed out at a second line parade as a memorial. Drawing donated by Helen Regis.

Kim Groves

Kim Groves lived around the corner. I used to call her Bright Eyes, because she had these very beautiful brown eyes. Her death was a tragedy because a person lost their life for doing the right thing. She reported police brutality and was killed for it. We martyred her for being a person who stood for the right thing and gave her life for it. Even though the powers that be who caused her death thought her life didn't have any meaning, to the people in the community it did. After we memorialized Kim, we decided to always recognize the losses in our community, regardless of whether they paraded with the Big Nine.

Joseph "Shotgun Joe" Williams

Joe was Betty Ann Lastie's grandson, the nephew of Herlin Riley, Jr., and a trumpet player for the Hot 8 Brass Band. It was a tragedy the way that he lost his life. It was stolen away from him. The police said when they cornered him, he started ramming a police car with the truck he was driving. But he was boxed in. How could he ram anything if they got him bumper to bumper? And then he's getting out of the truck with his hands up in the air when they killed him.

Opposite page: Phonett Davis, the rope holder for the Nine Times parade in 2007, has also roped for the Big Nine and is now their banner carrier. Originally from the state of Florida, he moved to New Orleans two years before Katrina and now "feels like a native of the city for going through the storm." Explaining the role of the rope in a parade, which is used to separate the club members from the second line, he says, "Holding the rope is a great honor, but it's hard work. You got to know what you're doing and have to have some control. You got people who want to get inside the ropes to dance with the club, and we're there to keep them off the dancers. You got to keep them boxed in with the rope so they don't interfere with the line." Photograph by Rachel Breunlin.

In the Street

"We come coordinated together."

Eric Gardner [*center*], who was born and raised in the Florida Public Housing Development, dances with other club members from Nine Times Social and Pleasure Club. Eric explains how his club decides on routines, "On parade day, we'll say a prayer and talk about what we should do along our route. Club members make suggestions and then we'll vote on it—the majority of votes rules. Everyone likes to dance by themselves to show off their own moves, but when we stop the parade and the band keeps playing, we know what we have to do. We might get in a single line, holding our canes up in the air. Or we might form a circle, like we're doing in this picture. The crowd on the other side of the rope comes to see you dance. They'll really be pumping you up, yelling, 'Do your thing!' It be exclusive." Photograph by Rachel Breunlin.

They say that a second line parade is a big dance party in the street, but there is a lot of preparation that goes into making it happen, and the responsibilities don't end when the parade begins.

Years ago, clubs paraded all day, but now the city restricts them to four hours. The club needs a plan for getting through the entire route on time. The grand marshall leads the parade and oversees that everything goes right. The parade chairman is the working fella moving up and down the parade making sure that everybody follows that law. He or she tells you its time to come out of the bar when the parades is about to begin, blows that whistle, and says, "Come on, you got to go—we're on a schedule, keep moving." During the parade the parade chairman is corresponding with the police, the club, and the band. The whole nine yards.

The clubs use the rope to maintain order on the streets because people who follow the second line get so involved in all the activity, they end up in the middle of your parade where the club members are dancing.

Some supporters of the club will ask, "Can I hold the ropes for y'all?" In all goodness, most clubs will give them some kind of stipend for helping. It's a hard job maintaining order. You need to know the decorum. If people get in your parade, you just tap them and tell them, "Hey, you got to get on the side." Most of the time, if you use that decorum, they're gonna acknowledge that.

The Sideline

You can't tell the story of a parade without the people who follow it. They are such an interactive part of the event. As a club, you got people from all walks of life coming together for that common cause of parading down the street. Those outside of the ropes come together for the same common cause—having fun on the streets of New Orleans.

The sideliners love to second line. You can see the ones who dance on the sidewalk putting on the great street performances. They love to climb on roofs and jump on top of cars, do sommersaults and splits. Oh, yeah. Every week, they'll be tearing it down.

There are people who faithfully follow certain clubs, and then there are people who follow certain brass bands. You will see them with that band, playing tambourines and cowbells, and blowing whistles. They become a part of that band during the parades even though they're not officially members.

Top: Ronny Slim dances on top of a church on Caffin and Galvez in the Lower Ninth Ward during a Big Nine parade. Photograph donated by Robert "Big Bob" Starks. Big Bob says, "He's good for climbing on top of buildings. Ever since we started, he's been following us. It's his chance to showcase his dancing. We try to get him to parade, but he always follows. Many people are religious about it." *Center:* Second liners bring their own musical instruments, including tambourines and empty glass pints, to walk behind the band at the Dumaine Gang parade in 2008. Photograph by Rachel Breunlin. *Bottom:* Ronny Slim dances at the Big Nine's 2006 parade in the Lower Ninth Ward in an overgrown lot. Photograph by Andy Levin.

A second line crowd dances to the music of the Olympia Brass Band. Photograph by Jules Cahn, courtesy of the Historic New Orleans Collection.

Tempo

If you look at *All on a Mardi Gras Day* and see how those people were second lining in the 1960s and 70s, the style of dance has changed to the rhythm of the music. Since the 1980s with the Dirty Dozen, Rebirth, New Birth, and now groups like the Hot 8 and the To Be Continued Brass Band, the music is more upbeat compared to bands like the Olympia and Eureka Brass Bands who played more traditional music. Back then, the movement of people was more flowing. They had a suavey type of style to the dance. Now, the band cranks it and the dancers are doing flips, splits, and handstands because the tempo of the music is faster and they're feeling the beat. The whole parade moves faster. The band you choose for your parade should represent the style of your club.

The To Be Continued Brass Band's tuba player can be seen in the midst of a sea of people following the Second Line Task Force's Renew New Orleans second line on January 15, 2006. The intensity of the interaction between the music and the second line always skyrockets with the amazing acoustics under the N. Claiborne Bridge. Kalamu ya Salaam writes, "When people dance to second line music, they look like a contraction. The music doesn't follow the twos and fours like most popular dance music. The rhythms aren't there just to frame out the melodies and harmonies. In a way, the rhythms are the whole thing. The rhythm does what it wants. The sudden twists and shifts of the music cause the dancers to do sudden twists and shifts of their own. The best dancers have a way of merging jerking with gliding."[20] Photograph by Rachel Breunlin. *Next Spread:* Nine Times lead their second line up the Almonaster Bridge in the Ninth Ward in 2007. At a parade, the closer you are to the club and the band, the more you'll have to keep up with the beat of the music, and dance. Walking in front of or behind the nucleus of the parade, the crowd spreads out and there is enough room to talk and catch up with friends. Photograph by Rachel Breunlin.

What You're Working With

Left to right: The Sixth Ward Diamonds and the Jolly Bunch parading with signature parade regalia. CEO of the Original Four Social & Pleasure Club and parade designer Kevin Dunn explains the importance of artwork and color coordination: "The art of the second line is the beauty of the second line. Beautiful decorations draw people to it. That's what they look for—just like suits are the biggest part of the Indians." Photographs by Jules Cahn from 1969, courtesy of the Historic New Orleans Collection.

Choosing colors and regalia add to our parades. When it's all put together, it says, "Here we come."

Second line clubs are competitive and other clubs want to see what you're working with—what you're bringing to the streets on that Sunday. It's up to you to bring out your best. When deciding on colors and regalia for your club, you want to make sure the look fits your organization. You don't want a bunch of mature men looking like teenage boys.

Years ago, when clubs like the Jolly Bunch paraded, you had various divisions with different regalia. One carried baskets, one had umbrellas. It's exciting and colorful. You parade up the street, and everybody's calling your name,

wanting to take a picture with you with your fancy suit. A cigar in your mouth, hat ace deuce. Stick your feet out and show them a beautiful

Red leather shoes worn for a Big Nine parade in 1999. Photograph courtesy of Beverly Kunze Photography.

The Second Division of the Big Nine parades in 2004 in red leather suits. Ronald is in the middle, and his wife, Minnie, is behind him on the left holding up an umbrella. Photograph donated by Robert "Big Bob" Starks.

pair of shoes. You are signifying, *Before I go back to the normal life, I am the big shot for a day.*

When it comes to making regalia, some things, like banners, are meant to last for years, while others can only be used once. We don't recycle streamers, baskets, umbrellas and fans because they are meant to be created for a particular year's theme. Many clubs make their own regalia, but others, especially when they're first starting out, might ask people known for creative designs from other clubs or Mardi Gras Indian tribes to help them.

Clubs get into the themes of what are going on at the time. I remember when the R&B singer Teddy Pendergrass was hot. He wore cowboy boots and a cowboy hat, and one club dressed like that in their parade.

By the Big Nine being a very mature group of men, we don't really go too far off the line. The colors we choose for our parades are usually subdued—navy blue and the powder blue, a two-piece brown suit. We want to look distinguished. We're not young boys, we're fully grown men with grown children. But parading is like the Mardi Gras Indians in a way—you want an element of surprise and to do something differently than other clubs. In 2004, my division surprised the culture when we wore these two- piece red leather suits. They were like, "Goddamn, look at these old soldiers there. Look at them old hot boys."

Ernest Lee was the banner carrier for the Big Nine Social & Pleasure Club for years. The banner was made by the Pennant Shop, Inc. on Old Metairie Road. Photograph donated by Robert "Big Bob" Starks.

Banners

Banners signify who you are and tell your history. They can include when your club was incorporated, who is an officer, what your motto is, or memorialize a deceased member. In a parade, banners are part of the front line, and clubs need to find a banner man to carry it throughout the parade. It has to be someone who won't leave it on the ground because, for us, our banner is just like carrying the American flag. You've got to carry it with respect.

There are some lively banner men who are known for their dancing. They had this great banner man called Gilbert Hatley. Gilbert was a Mardi Gras Indian and a member of the Zulu Social Aid & Pleasure Club. He carried banners for almost every club uptown, and when he died and they had his jazz funeral, clubs from across the city brought their banners out to remember his legacy.

Top left: The Popular Ladies' banner includes their logo and the commandment, "Thou Shall Not Kill," which speaks back to the struggles against violence in neighborhoods around New Orleans. Aquilla Journee elaborates, "Our logo is the boot—it represents classy ladies stepping out in style. Not killing and fighting, but showing your footwork. You want to go out there and dance." Photograph by Rachel Breunlin. *Top right:* The Original New Orleans Lady Buck Jumpers with their banner at Jazz Fest. Their president, Linda Porter, explains their motto, "On the Wall": "It means we're always ready. When it's time for us to hit the street, our clothes are ready. We don't have to second guess it. We're

ready to come out whatever day the parade is." Photograph taken from the route sheet from their 2006 parade. *Bottom right:* Sudan Social & Pleasure Club's logo signfies the Pan-African parading connections by featuring the continent of Africa with parade regalia. Coach Teedy says, "Old parades always had an umbrella, a basket, and a fan. In the 25 years we've paraded, we've always had all three." Photograph by Lindsey Darnell. *Bottom left:* Joe Spot, Grand Marshall of the Young Men Olympian Junior Benevolent Association, stands with their banner. It includes their motto, "In Unity, In Strength," as well as the years the club organized and incorporated. Photograph donated by Joe Spot.

An umbrella designed by Melvin Reed for a Popular Ladies parade was donated to the museum by club member Aquilla Journee. Melvin Reed, well known for his Indian suit designs, is also a master at parade regalia. He got his start with the Bucket Men, a Seventh Ward club begun by Jerome Smith. Melvin remembers, "Their parade was the first second line I saw. Allison Montana had a big old basket he made and sat it in front of the car. I started working with Jerome, creating umbrellas, fans, and streamers for the club. We used to make baskets that looked like bass drums, French Quarter buggies, and hearts. We make them with cardboard and hot glue." Since his days with Tambourine and Fan and the Bucket Men, he has mentored a number of people in the craft, including Coach Teedy. He chuckles as he remembers, "Teedy came out of our workshop. He was an excellent student." Today, Melvin works on designs for the Black Men of Labor and other clubs like the Popular Ladies who seek his services. Photograph by Devin Meyers of Fotos for Humanity.

Baskets

Left: Photograph of baskets at a Sudan parade, donated to the museum by Kenneth "Dice" Dykes. *Right:* Parade regalia is made by Adrian "Coach Teedy" Gaddies. He is shown here holding one of his baskets from the club's 2007 parade. A co-founder of Sudan, Coach Teedy says, "There are not many guys that actually make stuff and parade. I'm an artist, but I parade. I was 12 years old when I was introduced to it. I started as a young guy parading with Tambourine and Fan and learned from Melvin Reed. He started teaching us how to make fans. As a teenager, I started experimenting with it to see what I could come up with.

"This is a craft, and I believe in stating where the art comes from. It didn't come from me. It comes from somewhere. I can actually say the work I've been doing for 25 years comes from Melvin. I don't claim to be a person that owns it. I was taught it and made it my own." Photograph by Lindsey Darnell.

Opposite page: Dumaine Gang flag, donated by the club. The fans are made by Coach Teedy. Byron Hogans, president of the Dumaine Gang, says, "It's a pride thing to have some of the prettiest fans of the season. We might have a design in mind, but we don't want to tie Coach Teedy's hands. He's gifted and talented and we want to let him use his creativty." Photograph courtesy of Beverley Kunze Photography. *Above:* Gus Lewis comes out of the Tremé Center during the Dumaine Gang's parade. He says, "They always say I'm booted up when I come out the door. You'll see my best steps. I tune into one the instruments, grab that beat, and it pumps me up. The crowd's cheering me on, calling out, 'Put those shoes on that block!' 'Stump that ground!' 'Monkey shine!' They're looking for a little dance that I do where I smack the ground with my feet. Sometimes I like to have two fans in my hand going in opposite directions. I like rocking with them or waving to the rhythm the music gives me. I can use them as a shield against the sun or to let the crowd know they need to back up so I can do a move." Photograph by Andy Levin.

Fans

The fan goes back to benevolent societies and churches before the days of air conditioning. It evolved with everything else. For something that was very, very simple to something that has their own type of creative genius in it, to represent your club.

To make a fan, you first begin by drawing up the design. Cut the wood to make the size and shape of the fan, and then bring material to the printing shop to make a screen for your print. Once you have the design printed, come back and put it all together with feathers to accent it. The parade fans you see with the feathers and the trims that they use today comes from Mardi Gras Indian designs.

On the street, social and pleasure clubs dance with the fans—they're styling, profiling. Just like an Indian suit, those little plumes are waving in the air. It's mesmerizing. When you're two blocks away and looking in the direction of that parade, the first thing you see in the air is the color of those fans.

Members of Black Men of Labor Social Aid and Pleasure Club in front of Sweet Lorraine's on St. Claude Avenue in the Seventh Ward. Fred Johnson says it's important to the club to make a statement about, "the origins of the culture of second lines—their connections to Africa. It's not an accident that we parade on Sundays—the day slaves were able to congregate in Congo Square, the day when Mardi Gras Indians practice. The parades are part of a lineage of African retentions. That's why we wear a combination of Senegalese and European outfits with umbrellas." For many years, Allison "Tootie" Montana designed Black Men of Labor's parade regalia. Photograph by Ronald W. Lewis.

Umbrellas

The umbrellas go back to West Africa. In many villages, the tribal chief would come out on a given day and lead a procession. His authority would be signified by an umbrella.[21] In New Orleans, social and pleasure clubs use them in a similar way—to show off our prestige for the day. For a long time, second liners brought umbrellas to the parade, too, but this trend has come and gone.

Edgar Jacobs, Big Chief of the Choctaw Hunters, dancing in a Big Nine Social & Pleasure Club parade in 2006. He was inspired to make umbrellas, he says, by "my two heroes, Matthew 'Black' Brock and Jerome Smith. When I was growing up, Black Brock was a well-known figure in the neighborhood. He used to sing behind Tom Sparks and the Yellow Jackets—he had a golden voice. Every year, he paraded with the Sixth Ward High Steppers and decorated an umbrella with ribbon and baby dolls.

"When I got older, I started parading with the Bucket Men. Jerome wanted to bring the Seventh Ward up. They had the Sixth Ward High Steppers, the Tremé Diamonds, the Tremé Sports, but it wasn't nothing in the Seventh Ward." The social and pleasure clubs in the Ninth Ward got their start for a similar reason, with the Bucket Men's legacy showing up in the elaborate umbrellas Edgar makes each year. Photograph by Andy Levin.

Left: A peach and brown streamer made by Kevin Dunn for his club, the Original Four's, second line parade in October 2007 incorporates multiple components of a well–designed streamer. When it is worn, the sash across the chest will showcase the name of the club on one side, and the name of the club member on the other. Underneath is the parade's theme, taken from a popular song, "Wipe Me Down," which celebrates looking good: In the song, Lil Foxx and Lil Boosie call out, "Shoulders, chest, pants, shoes. Cause I'm on, Wipe me down." [22] Above the rhinestone lettering is a club member literally being wiped down by an admiring woman.

Top: Kevin explains the originality of his work, "All my designs are created by me with my own style. I don't make no look–a–likes. I have guys that are willing to let me do my thing and put money up for it. As far as the sash part, I use expensive material—velvet. I use ribbon, satin, embroidery and rhinestones to accent it. A lot of the Indians pay attention to my work. We share the same work ethic because most of it is all hands. That's what made me start to use rhinestones—seeing it on Indians' costumes." Photographs by Lindsey Darnell.

Streamers/Sashes

Sashes are the badge of honor you wear. If you have your organization's name running across your chest, BIG NINE SOCIAL & PLEASURE CLUB, and you come out there dancing and flipping, you'll just swell up: *This is who I am: Big Nine.*

A lot of clubs put the theme of their parade on their streamers, too. In the late 1990s, the rapper Master P's daddy started the No Limit Social and Pleasure Club, and the theme of their club was the tank. They put a line from one of his most popular hits, "Bout Dat" on their streamers— "Bling Bling."

Kevin Dunn, at his workshop in his house, reflects on his history of parading, designing, and mentorship. Mr. Harold "Dynamite" Featherson, the former Big Chief of the White Cloud Hunters, "was somewhat of a mentor to me. I'd go to his house and just watch. Then I started working on my first streamer. When I brought it back to Dynamite, he told me that once I learned how to sew on a sewing machine, there'd be no stopping me, 'You on your way now. Boy, you gonna be bad!' He saw something I didn't see in myself. 2009 will be 30 years that I did my own group's decorations."

Over the years, Kevin has worked with the West Bank Steppers, Lady Buck Jumpers, Lady Sequins, VIP Ladies, Mahogany Ladies, Ladies of Essence, Keepin it Real, Pigeon Town Steppers, Revolution, Family Ties, and Good Fellas. He credits his best friend, Wendell Jackson, for encouraging him to branch out. "It took me years to get to where I am now and doing things more easily. I went from making decorations on the street to getting involved in the Folklife area of Jazz Fest and making decorations for musicians like Wanda Rouzan and Cyril Neville. One time I made sashes for Miller Beer with Miller cans at the top."

After Katrina, Kevin lived in Dallas for two years. "One of the guys from CTC Steppers named Andrew called to see if I would still do their decorations for their parade. I told him I didn't have no more tools to do their work. He said he would supply all the tools for me. He gave me a push to come back, and after I saw all the love from the groups, it made me want to start doing their work for them again. I have two guys who I mentor—Arnold Ray and Terrence Williams. Without their help, I wouldn't do all the things I do with other clubs." He gets most of his supplies from Jefferson Variety and works with the Pennant Shop to do the embroidery, "I might create it, but it can't get done without Jack. We work it out until we get it to the level we want it."

The Pennant Shop opened in 1932, and the family has worked with social and pleasure clubs for years. Jack Matranga says, "We don't advertise it—one group will just tell another through word of mouth. Anybody can cut a letter out of felt and glue it on. We made it an art form. The embroidery looks more professional—it gives a more finished, expensive look."

Most of the embroidery is done on a freehand Singer embroidery machine that is about 100 years old. "I think we're the only ones in the state that use it. The man that designed it was a genius. Wherever my hands go, that's where the machine goes. My wife says, 'It's like painting with thread.' Like an artist uses paint, I use thread.

"I'm the only one who uses it. You have to grow up in it like I did. I started out when I was about 14 and I haven't missed a day of work in 40 years. You have to know how to work it and how to repair it. There's nobody around to fix them. It's a dedication and you have to love it. It's a very unique business. It's labor– intensive. Sometimes I work 16 hours a day. If something happens to me, there might not be any more lettering." Photographs by Lindsey Darnell.

Top: Keepin It Real members parading down N. Claiborne in 2007, wearing streamers made by Kevin Dunn. Photograph by Ronald W. Lewis. *Right:* A close–up of the streamer. The club's theme in 2007, "We Fly, No Lie. We Ballin," came from "We Fly High," a song taken from Jim Jones' third album, *Hustler's P.O.M.E. (Product of My Environment)*. In the song, Jones sings, "We fly high, no lie, you know this (Ballin)." Keepin It Real's incorporation of the popular song into their parade isn't the only time it took on a more local flavor—New Orleans rapper Lil Wayne's remix of "We Fly High" calls out the city's area code: "We stay high on that 5–0–4 shit (New Orleans!)" [23] While Keepin It Real's themes often showcase hip–hop's flashier side, in their prayers before meetings and in their motto, "The more we hustle, the more we have," they underscore that the beauty of their parades is based on hard work. Photograph by Rachel Breunlin.

Keepin It Real Social & Pleasure Club at Club Good Times. *Front Row:* Gaynelle Butler, Perry Franklin, Kimberley Cureaux (Keepin It Real's 2009 Queen), Kobin Wright. *Back Row:* Rodney Green, Charles "Buster" Spencer, Michael "Disco" Valdery, Kenneth "Stepper" McDonalds, Richard Brown, Dondi Franklin, and Harry Picot.

The social and pleasure club was started by Perry Franklin, Michael "Disco" Valdery, and Kobin Wright after parading for years with the Young Men Olympian and Revolution. The business manager, Gaynelle Butler, says, "It ain't no uptown/downtown thing. We're from all over the city."

Each generation of social and pleasure clubs brings a new way of understanding the nature of representation and identity to the streets. As the author of *Hip Hop Philosophy*, Marcyliena Morgan, argues, "The hip hop mantra 'keepin it real' represents the quest for the [coming together] of ever-shifting art, politics, representation, performance and individual accountability." [24] In 2006, their parade's regalia represented their commitment to rebuilding to New Orleans: "N.O. 4-Ever." Photographs by Rachel Breunlin.

Part V

Skeletons

A skeleton head made by Brian Bush of Carnival Sculpture. Growing up in Gretna, Louisiana, he started making paper maché piñatas when he was ten years old, and later worked for many of the major Mardi Gras float and decorating businesses—Kern, Royal, T&A. Although he lived across the river, Brain says, "I always spent Fat Tuesday uptown with my uncle. One Mardi Gras morning, when I was about nine, we went down Claiborne Avenue to deliver a costume. At one intersection, a small second line stopped traffic for several minutes. My uncle and godmother were focused on the band and dancers, but I saw something else down the street. It was a skeleton!!! A bloody skeleton with a big bloody bone!!! He seemed to be pointing at me. It scared me. It thrilled me. I loved it. Carnival was in my blood. This just reaffirmed it."

Ronald and Brian met in 2002 at the New Orleans Jazz & Heritage Festival's Folklife Village. "After the flood, I heard of the massive effort to help Ronald rebuild. I know that donating this 'skull' is a small gesture, but it was what I could do at the time." The skull, made out of cardboard and paper maché was sculpted with the help of an old bicycle helmet. The hanging ropes of hair, Brian says, "are actually made of cheese cloth, which is light, looks creepy, and moves a lot. It also was made during my flood line phase, when everything I did was tattered below the flood line." Photograph by Devin Meyers of Fotos for Humanity.

From the Royce Osborne Film *All on a Mardi Gras Day.*[1]

Allison "Tootie" Montana: Mardi Gras day long time ago before World War II, the first people you see on the street is the Indian and skulls.

Miriam Reed: We were in the house and my momma said, "Here come the skeletons!" Everybody looking 'round, go under the bed, get in the closet, hide in the bathroom, or somewhere. But they were something frightful to look at.

Al Morris: When we would travel, we'd go to different houses and wake up the neighborhood, cause we'd get out before dark, before daylight. But we carry tambourines, cowbells, something to make noise, so when we're going through on Mardi Gras morning, everybody can hear the noise...They knew Mardi Gras ain't Mardi Gras without seeing them bone gangs.

INTRODUCTION
Skeletons
By Helen A. Regis

All on a Mardi Gras Day, the first in-depth documentary to portray New Orleans Black Mardi Gras, aired on public television in 2003. It is the best oral history of the role of Skeletons in New Orleans carnival. The filmmaker, Royce Osborn, grew up in the Seventh Ward, not too far away from N. Claiborne Avenue—the epicenter of Black carnival before the construction of the interstate highway overpass in the 1960s. Before he began researching the topic, he says, "I vaguely had an ancient memory of skeletons on the street at Mardi Gras, but I might have repressed it completely because it was too scary and weird." The story of the making of his film is a great example of how documentary work can be more than a witness, but also generate cultural production itself. The movie helped recharge the old-time Mardi Gras—not just the Bones, but the Baby Dolls who often paraded with them. Royce says,

> After the movie first came out, we started really seeing a revival of the Baby Dolls. There were a couple dozen Baby Dolls in 2004. They all came out of the Mother-in-Law Lounge on N. Claiborne. After that year, they split into rival factions, so I knew it was gonna be strong.

Royce recalls how Miriam Reed [*second to left*] gave, "a Baby Doll seminar to show how to make the costumes. Miriam would say, 'Well, I like to have Scotch and milk in my bottle but you can drink anything you want.' Then she got to really show them how to do the walk, the dance, and how to roll with being a Baby Doll." Photograph by Royce Osborn.

The original Baby Doll revival was spearheaded by Mrs. Miriam Batiste Reed, who was one of the oldest surviving Baby Dolls. Raised up in the Sixth Ward in a musical family, she recalled how her entire family made costumes and came out as baby dolls with the Original Dirty Dozen Kazoo Band.[2]

Mrs. Reed sewed several Baby Doll costumes on her sewing machine in the traditional manner and several other women designed their own takes on the strange sexy baby doll dresses and bonnets—their own fertility symbols. Seen together, the Skeletons and the Baby Dolls remind us of the cycle of life.

The North Side Skull and Bones Gang in front of Ernie K-Doe's Mother-in-Law lounge on Mardi Gras Day, 2004. Photograph by Royce Osborn.

Multiple images of Gédé, mitigator of life and death, healer of the sick and escort of the dead to the other side, are found on Vodou flags created by sequin artists in Haiti. The flags each include his colors (purple, black, and white) and, according to Tina Girouard, evoke "glowing stained glass windows in Catholic churches and the shimmering sequin art found in Vodou temples." To make a flag, "the eight mm sequins are held in place by a glass bead: the needle guides the threat through the fabric, then through the sequin, the bead, and finally... to the cloth. A typical artwork requires an artisan to attach 18-20 thousand sequins, a feat accomplished in about ten days." *Left:* Anotine Oleyant's Vodou flag depicts Baron La Croix, a Gédé spirit, standing on a coffin. Oleyant became a sequin artist when Erzulie Freda, the lwa of love, visited him and promised to show him how to create art that would take care of him for the rest of his life. Tragically, he died of a stroke when he was only 39 years old. Photograph courtesy of Indigo Arts Gallery. *Center:* Another Gédé image by Antoine depicts the lwa standing on a tombstone inside a bottle of rum, the spirit's favorite libation. Above is a pink circle representing the all—seeing eye. To the right is an *asson*, the sacred rattle of a Vodou priest, and a bell. Surrounding the bottle are the three sacred drums and two snakes representing the lwa Damballa. *Right:* A collaboration between the Louisiana artist Tina Girouard and the Haitian sequin artist George Valris. For over a decade, Tina maintained a studio in Port-au-Prince, collaborating with both Antoine and George. From 1987 to the present, Tina has organized exhibitions of sequin art in New Orleans and across the United States. [3]

Skeletons Cross Culturally

Perhaps no other mask reduces human experience to its essential core like the skeleton. Around the world, their use in masquerades honors the dead, comforts the bereaved, and connects us with those who came before. But they can also express bawdy truths and poke fun at pretensions of the powerful and the hypocrisy of the pieties of the day. Throughout the Caribbean and Latin America, as well as Africa, they are widespread carnival costumes. Bruce Barnes, a musician, National Park Service ranger, and member of the Black Men of Labor, participates in Skeleton masking tradition in New Orleans and has studied the history of carnival traditions. In Royce's film, he points to the connections between skeletons in New Orleans and Haiti, explaining that

The Second Chief of the North Side Skull and Bones Gang, Bruce "Sunpie" Barnes, wears a top hat the evokes the presence of Baron Samdi, another incarnation of Gédé.

perhaps the tradition came to New Orleans with the Haitians who emigrated to the city in the late 1700s and early 1800s:

> Certainly you see almost the exact same costume in terms of the skeleton here in New Orleans' Skeleton gangs, and what you see in Haiti. The lwa Gédé, which is a guardian of the cemetery, is very, very strongly preserved here…He is associated with death, the skeleton itself, and fertility. He's very rambunctious, he's over sexually active . . . [Some would] say Gédé controls the whole thing… Gédé is everywhere that has anything to do with Mardi Gras, and the skeletons are a wake-up call for what's happening and what's going to happen.[4]

In Haiti, Gédé is the spirit who rules over the popular carnival, an event centered around marching bands called *bann apye* (groups on foot). As in New Orleans, Haitian middle classes worry about how outsiders might view their

Members of the North Side Skull and Bones Gang in front of John Ferrara's meat market in Tremé. Al Morris recalls, "Everybody had a bone. The bloodier it was, the more meat it had on it, the better it looked, you know what I'm saying?" Photograph by Wayne Ferrara, donated by Royce Osborn.

popular festivities, seeing "carnival disorder…as a blight on Haiti's reputation."[5] Concerns around respectability and control extend throughout the Caribbean and in New Orleans. Calypso star and historian Hollis "Chaldust" Liverpool writes that in Trinidad, Africans controlled the streets during the carnival season as Europeans and free people of color retreated to private balls and house parties.[6] In the same way, middle-class and respectable African Americans in New Orleans at times have sought to distance themselves from black popular festivals, including second line parades and the masquerades of the Skeletons, Baby Dolls, and Mardi Gras Indians.

In the early 20th century Haiti, elites introduced a "bourgeois-style carnival patterned on French and Italian prototypes which was meant to subordinate and undermine a popular festivity."[7] This European style Mardi Gras with floats and elegant pageantry is similar to the elite carnival of floats and tableaux started by white New Orleanians in the 1850s—the Mardi Gras of Comus and Rex was an effort to reclaim the streets for the New Orleans elite who disapproved of the popular masquerades that brought people together on the streets of the city.

But the popular expressions of freedom still continue in many forms throughout the African diaspora. In Trinidad, they may be traced to the 19th century Canne Brulee (canboulay) freedom celebrations that initially commemorated emancipation, on August 1, 1834. Amongst the masqueraders were skeletons. In the 1840s, one African wore "a skeleton painted on a coal-black shape, walked about with part of a horse's vertebra attached to him and a horse's thigh bone in his hand."[8] Sound familiar?

A Day of the Dead altar in 2004 hosted by Mano a Mano: Mexican Culture Without Borders, a nonprofit based in New York City and dedicated to promoting the understanding of Mexican traditions among immigrants, artists, educators, and the general public. Photograph courtesy of Mano a Mano.

The Skeleton as Social Equalizer

Many Aztec deities were represented with skulls in stone sculptures, including Coatlicue, "the goddess of earth, life, and death, whose face usually appears as a skull." [9] Mictecacihuatl, goddess of death and co-ruler, with her husband, of the underworld, was worshipped by the Aztecs. The Spanish brought their own skeleton traditions, and attempted to wipe out indigenous religions. Despite repression by the Catholic Church, popular death rites continued through colonial times

into the modern era. The skeleton is a prominent guest at Mexican Day of the Dead festivities today, making appearances as sugar candy, sculptures, toys, and in papel picados (paper banners). Calaveras, mock epitaphs, prose poems, and etchings composed for the occasion, serve as powerful social critique and satire:

It will be a great equality
that levels big and small
There will be neither poor nor rich
in that society

In this widening world,
Gold perverts everyone
But after death
There are neither classes nor rank [10]

Reminders of death and struggle can jar us out of our day-to-day comforts. The fear that Skeletons brought to New Orleanians was a reminder of the potency of life, as well as the inevitability of death. This disruption is similar to rituals Margaret Drewal has observed in the Nigerian city of Abeokuta. During certain occasions, men who put on warrior masks frighten people as the Indians and Skeletons did in New Orleans. Drewal writes,

> Warrior masks are turned loose to run rampant throughout the town from their separate households...They are followed by small armies of young men who grab all sorts of things in their paths and throw them...The townspeople stampede to escape confrontation...Part of the drama of the warrior masks is their sudden intrusions into public spaces where people work and live. People know that it is the time when warrior masks are out and about but the precise moment of confrontation is unexpected. [11]

Left: Although rare, there are other pockets of Skeletons around the city besides the North Side Skull and Bones Gang. In the Seventh Ward of New Orleans, Derek Meilleur began making skeleton heads in the late 1980s when his uncle, Ronald "Buck" Baham, began masking as a Mardi Gras Indian. He says, "I used to see them on Claiborne. On Mardi Gras, my mom and them were deadly afraid of them. After I started making them, I found out after that my daddy had made them, too. And my great uncle—he made them with wire. I was making them with a balloon because I didn't know. I found a piece of wire and I shaped it. I made it like me—my own bone structure. I closed my eyes to do it. It's a feeling. If I was blind I could do it. When you put on the mask, you feel different. You are that thing. I think about it right now. It's death. I'm even afraid of it. Do you believe that?" *Center:* Derek masks with the Seventh Ward Warriors on Mardi Gras Day 2005. *Right:* The skeleton mask is passed around throughout the day. Derek says, "If kids tried to run from me, I take the head off and show them it's a person underneath it. It's all right. I make them come shake my hand, take pictures." Photographs by Rachel Breunlin.

Like the Skeletons, the warrior masks get a key part of their costumes from the butcher shop: bones, meat and the fearsome smell of rotting meat are part of the performance.

What's Ahead

Ronald's involvement with the North Side Skull and Bones Gang began with his retirement, and has developed alongside the building of his museum. His work as a documenter and as a participant of the gang attempts to keep the Bones in the street. Other members, such as Royce Osborn, Bruce Barnes, and Michael Crutcher have their feet in both worlds, too. Michael is a cultural geographer whose work focuses on the history of Tremé, the home of the North Side Skull and Bones' Chief, Al Morris.

Their home base at the Backstreet Cultural Museum, housed in a former Blandin Funeral Home, provides a good model to follow, as it nurtures contemporary traditions while maintaining an extensive archive. Every Carnival, people from around the world stop by on Mardi Gras day to see Mardi Gras Indians and Skeletons, to study African diaspora history, and, perhaps, to join in the dance.

Royce Osborne recalls a story about Al Morris: "For years he would mask as a Skeleton on Mardi Gras day. People would ask, 'Where's the rest of your tribe?' and Al would always say, 'They're comin.' Although no one was was following behind him, he knew eventually others would want to mask again." Photograph courtesy of Sylvester Francis and the Backstreet Cultural Museum.

You Next

Top: During Mardi Gras in 1962, John Ferrara took a number of slides of the Skull and Bones Gang in front of his meat market. John's son, Wayne Ferrara, gave the slides to Royce Osborn while Royce was working on *All on a Mardi Gras Day.* For kids without much money, masking with the legendary Big Arthur [*second from right*], who had masked as far back as the 1930s, was an alternative to the more expensive Mardi Gras Indian suits. Photograph donated by Royce Osborn.

Despite reports that Skeletons were a popular through the 1960s, tracking down images, as well as actual Skeleton Men, proved more difficult than Royce originally expected. He explains, "Finding the Skeleton Men was a real problem. I had heard about Al Morris, who's the Skeleton Chief of the North Side Skulls. Al had masked with Big Arthur. It took me weeks looking for Al Morris. I'd go to one corner, 'Have you see Al?' Well, you know, people didn't trust me. They didn't know who I was. I didn't have my New Orleans accent any more. So it's like the cops looking for him. They didn't give me shit."

Bottom: Chief Al in front of the Backstreet Museum with some of his skeleton heads. Royce continues, "I finally tracked him down at the Backstreet. Al's sitting on the steps looking at me with a big smile and going, 'I hear you've been lookin for me?' Yeah, for quite a while. And he's like, 'I wanted to make sure you were really serious about what you're doin.' If I'd given up he would have just said, "Eh, another fake.'

After I talked to Al, I decided I wanted to be a Skeleton. The idea of it just took hold of me. We came up with a Skeleton gang—my brother and I, a few friends of ours, and my little nephew. When I told Al we were gonna come, Al said, 'Oh, we'll wipe you off the street. We're gonna humiliate you and then we're gonna run you into the dirt.'

"We came out and went to the Backstreet looking for Al. When he finally showed up, he said we looked like shit. But he was all alone, he didn't have a gang with him, and although he thought we looked terrible, he let us follow him all through Tremé and the Seventh Ward and up to Orleans Avenue. It was my greatest Mardi Gras of all, and ever since then I've been a Skeleton Man." Photograph by Sylvester Francis courtesy of the Backstreet Cultural Museum.

Before Katrina, I started hanging out around the Backstreet—just Mardi Gras masking. One year, I dressed up in overalls, a flannel shirt, and hat, and I called myself a New Orleans Redneck. I had my face painted white and everything. While I was over there, I kept watching the North Side Skull and Bones Gang. There used to be Skeletons out every carnival, but they went into a decline, and it's been a few years since they've had a presence on the streets.

The makeup of the Bone Gang is basically similar to a Mardi Gras Indian gang. It's a tribal setup and the pecking order goes from the front to the back. Al Morris is the Chief, and Bruce "Sunpie" Barnes is the Second Chief. I said, "That looks like fun, and something I can retire into." I've been doing it for four years now. We have other members, including Stiltwalker, Royce Osborn, and Michael Crutcher.

I'm the gatekeeper. As the tribe travels, I'm the protector of our house. You come, I welcome you, or I turn you away. It's like the Gang Flag in a Mardi Gras Indian gang—as you finish moving through all the walls to meet the Big Chief, you have to meet the Gang Flag—he's the final layer before you meet the Big Chief.

Being the gatekeeper, I meet others as they come in the area of the Backstreet. My staff is part of the imagery. I tell them who I am and chat with them a little bit. Where you from? Where you goin? Children have that look of curiosity and some the look of fear about Skeletons. Then they have those that want to tear your skeleton head off. They don't have fear!

Ronald W. Lewis with his gatekeeper's staff, courtesy of Aubrey Edwards.

Skull and Bones gangs are another face of Mardi Gras that moved through Latin America and the Caribbean to New Orleans. People think it represents death, but it actually represents life because those bones were somebody. In our Bone Gang, we talk about the violence in the streets. We tell the kids, "If you're messing with drugs, there's a good chance you're next. You will be a skeleton if you don't do the right thing."

Since I started masking, I've collected some of the paper maché heads and other parts of the skull and bones costumes that go with them. Photographers have also donated images of the gang during carnival, and shared their own experiences with the Skeletons. It all helps tell the story.

Spread: In 2008, Ronald was asked by Andy Levin, a photographer and frequent contributor to the House of Dance & Feathers, to talk at a photography workshop Andy was running called Mardi Gras 360 Degrees. Ronald talked to photographers both in and out of town about the ethics of photographing on the street. As a cautionary tale, he told the story of a photographer who got between two Mardi Gras Indian tribes who were meeting. Angling for the best shot, he lay on the ground and was stepped on by a Wildman.

One of the workshop participants listening to Ronald's talk was Charles Silver, a photographer based out of Louisville, Kentucky. He says, "After, I approached him and realized that we were the same age and had the same interests." Charles was planning on photographing Mardi Gras day. "I told Ronald 'Whatever you need, whoever you think I should shoot, I'll do it and provide prints.'"

He spent the morning with the North Side Skull and Bones Gang. "From Ronald, I have met the most incredible people. There so many photographs of New Orleans, the city. I'm really interested in the people—their faces, expressions, what they do. I try to show that in the photographs I take. The historic buildings should be documented, but the people and their stories is what also needs to be preserved." Photographs by Charles Silver.

While working on this book, Ronald and Rachel also served on the advisory board for the 6t'9 Social Aid & Pleasure Club, an organization founded after Katrina by L.J. Goldstein [*with umbrella*] and Ann Marie Coviello [*on bicycle*] to bridge the predominantly white, bohemian art world and the predominantly Black second line culture. Since 2005, their parade, beginning in the Sixth Ward and ending in the Ninth Ward, has invited people involved in both cultures to come together to celebrate Halloween. Their King-For-Life is Chief Al Morris [*sitting between Alton and Royce Osborn*]. In 2005 and 2006, the North Side Skull and Bones Gang joined scores of other Skeletons on the streets of downtown New Orleans.

In a booklet for the club in 2008, Ann Marie locates the work of 6t'9 as the traditions around Halloween and the Day of the Dead, as well as the zodiac sign Scorpio. According to Caroline Casey's *Making the Gods Work for You*, Scorpio represents "death; rebirth; transformation. The alchemy of desire. All initiations of descent into the Underworld. All things that are unseen: death, sex, spirits, ancestors." [12]

End Notes

Part I: Introduction

Portions of this essay were previously published in *Cornerstones: Celebrating the Everyday Monuments and Meeting Places of New Orleans' Neighborhoods*, published by the Neighborhood Story Project in 2008, and presented at the Southern Anthropological Society's 2008 conference in Staunton, Virginia with Helen Regis. Ronald's portions of the essay come from interviews conducted by Rachel Breunlin and Helen Regis from October 2005–November 2008. All other quotations come from interviews conducted in August–December 2008 by Rachel Breunlin, except for those with Eric Waters and Ada LeMann, which were edited from interviews by Lindsey Darnell.

1. Mardi Gras Indian tribes are groups of (usually) working class African American men in New Orleans who pay homage to American Indians on Mardi Gras day by dressing in elaborate, handmade, beaded costumes. Social aid and pleasure clubs are African American benevolent societies that host an annual participatory parade known as a second line. In these parades, the club welcomes spectators to walk or dance with them through their neighborhoods. For more information, see "Mardi Gras Indians" (p. 62) and "Social Aid and Pleasure Clubs" (p. 124) in this book.

For other sources, see Helen Regis' 1999 "Second Lines, Minstrelsy, and the Contested Landscapes of New Orleans Afro-Creole Festivals" in *Cultural Anthropology* 14:(4): 472-504; George Lipsitz's 1988 "Mardi Gras Indians: Carnival and Counter-Narrative in Black New Orleans" in *Cultural Critique* 10: 99–121; Joseph Roach's 1992 "Mardi Gras Indians and Others: Genealogies of

American Performance" in *Theatre Journal* 44 (4): 461–483; Michael P. Smith's 1994 *Mardi Gras Indians*, Gretna, LA: Pelican Publishing; and Jeffrey David Ehrenreich's 2004 "Bodies, Beads, Bones and Feathers: The Masking Tradition of Mardi Gras Indians in New Orleans—A Photo Essay" in *City & Society* 16 (1): 117–150.

A number of documentary films on Mardi Gras Indians have also made important contributions to the understanding of the performance traditions, including Maurice Martinez's 1976 *The Black Indians of New Orleans*, Les Blank's 1978 *Always for Pleasure*, Royce Osborn's 2003 *All on a Mardi Gras Day*, and Lisa Katzman's 2006 *Tootie's Last Suit*.

2. For more on the politics of identity and heritage in grassroots efforts like community museums, see James Clifford's 2004 "Looking Several Ways: Anthropology and Native Heritage in Alaska," in *Current Anthropology* 45 (1): 5–23. He writes, "[L]ike earlier anticolonial mobilizations, [they] complicate dichotomous, arguably Eurocentric conceptions of 'cultural' versus 'political' or 'economic' agency" (9).

3. In "What is this 'Black' in Black Popular Culture?," Stuart Hall writes, "Within the Black repertoire, *style*, which mainstream cultural critics often believe to be the husk, the wrapping...has become itself the subject of what is going on...[T]he people of the black diaspora.. have worked on ourselves as canvases of representation." The essay was published in 1998 as part of an excellent collection of essays called *Black Popular Culture: A Project by Michele Wallace* (Discussions in Contemporary Culture, Volume 8), edited by Gina Dent and organized by the Dia Foundation. New York: The New Press: 27.

For more on the tensions between embodied knowledge and documentary/archival work, see Diana Taylor's *The Archive and the Repertoire: Performing Cultural Memory in the Americas*, published by Duke University Press in 2003.

4. "The Painter as Photographer" by J. Lee Anderson in *The Mississippi Rag* August 1990: 1–5.

5. Ray Blazio's critique of documenters is not unusual. Looking at contemporary issues of cross-cultural representation, Clifford writes, "Indeed, 'the anthropologist'—broadly and sometimes stereotypically defined—has become a negative alter ego in contemporary indigenous discourse, invoked as the epitome of arrogant, intrusive colonial authority" (2004: 5).

6. Quoted in "Afterword" in Michael P. Smith's *Mardi Gras Indians*. For more on the violations that can occur in the photographer/subject relationship, see Susan Sontag's 1977 *On Photography*. New York: Anchor Book. Considering the sometimes one–sided nature of the medium, she says, "There is something predatory about taking a picture. To photograph people is to violate them, by seeing them as they never see themselves...it turns people into objects that can be symbolically possessed" (14).

7. In 1988, Andy Antippas curated an exhibit at the Icon Gallery in Houston called, "Ten Southern Black Folk Artists," which featured the work of Mardi Gras Indian Larry Bannock. The same year, *Caribbean Festival Arts: Each and Every Bit of Difference,* curated by John W. Nunley and Judith Bettelheim, was shown at the Saint Louis Art Museum and traveled to the Smithosonian Instituion, the Seattle Art Museum, and the Brooklyn Museum, among others. The exhibit featured Mardi Gras Indian suits and demonstrated links between the masking tradition in New Orleans, the Caribbean, and West Africa. Exhibits in New Orleans include "Mardi Gras: It's Carnival Time in Louisiana" on permanent display at the Louisiana State Museum and "He's the Prettiest: A Tribute to Big Chief Allison Montana's 50 Years of Mardi Gras Suiting," curated by Bill Fagaly in 1997 at the New Orleans Museum of Art (NOMA).

8. As Clifford points out, "Struggles over indigenous practice occur...'within and against' Western institutions and hegemonic ideas such as 'culture'" (2004: 14). Often times, community mueums are connected to larger institutions of power. The Backstreet Cultural Museum has collaborated with a number of well-endowed museums in the city to put on exhibitions. See, for example, "Mardi Gras Indians, Jazz Funerals, and Second Lines: Works from the Backstreet Cultural Museum" at the Ogden Museum of Southern Art, New Orleans from August-September 2006 and an exhibition of Victor Harris and the Spirit of Fi Yi Yi's work (on loan from the Backstreet), curated by Dan Cameron for Prospect.1, New Orleans at NOMA from November 2008–January 2009.

9. Jolie Préau 2003 *Sylvester Francis Representing the Back Streets: The Life History of a Man and His Museum*. Thesis, Master of Science in Urban Studies, Urban Anthropology, College of Urban and Public Affairs, University of New Orleans: 68.

10. For a discussion of the different technologies and media involved in street performances, see Helen Regis' 2001 "Blackness and the Politics of Memory in the New Orleans Second Line" in *American Ethnologist* 28(4): 757–777.

11. Among them are folklorist Joyce Jackson from Louisiana State University and cultural anthropologist Cheryl Ajirotutu from University of Wisconsin, Milwaukee, both of whom focus on the African Diaspora. UWM's Union Gallery hosted an exhibit of J. Nash Porter's photography of Mardi Gras Indians, "Contextual Portaits from an Insider's View" with accompanying writing by Joyce in January–February of 2007. The exhibit was originally on display at the Smithsonian's Anacostia Community Museum in Washington D.C. Ronald and Joyce gave a talk at the gallery

called, "Resistance Street Theatre: The Black Indians of Mardi Gras." Cheryl Ajirotutu has donated a mask to the museum from Senegal [*see above*].

12. See Joseph O. Palacio's 2005 edited volume, *The Garifuna, A Nation Across Borders: Essays in Social Anthropology.* Benque Viejo del Carmen, Belize: Cubola. Palacio donated numerous copies of this important book to the museum.

13. Quoted in *Freedom Dreams: The Black Radical Imagination*, by Robin D. G. Kelley, published by Beacon Press in 2003.

14. For more on developing histories through the use of photographs, see Alison K. Brown and Laura Peers with members of the Kainai Nation's 2007 *"Pictures Bring Us Messages, Sinaakssiiksi aohtsimaahpihkookiyaawa": Photographs and Histories from the Kainai Nation.* Toronto: University of Toronto Press. Reflecting on the process of repatriating the photographs, one of the Kainai participants, Louis Soop, said, "There is so much that goes on with these pictures. It's not just the person, there's a whole life history that they bring forth" (108).

Part II: The Lower Ninth Ward

Ronald's narratives come from interviews conducted by Rachel Breunlin and Helen Regis from October 2005–November 2008. All other quotations come from interviews conducted by Rachel Breunlin in August–November of 2008, except for those with Wayne Hill, Darryl Keys, and Glen David Andrews, which were edited from interviews by Lindsey Darnell.

1. See the Jackson Barracks Military Museum's website: http://www.la.ngb.army.mil/dmh/. Accessed on November 18, 2008.

2. Quoted from Will Sutton's "New Orleans' Lower Nine Fades, Fades, Fades Away" in *Nieman Reports* Winter 2005: 37.

3. Quoted from Samuel Beckett's 1954 *Waiting for Godot*. New York: Grove Press: 51.

4. In the two years we spent searching through archives for supporting images for this book, a common conversation with archivists, as well as other people doing research on the Lower Nine, was the lack of available background material. Interestingly, one of the main sources of images was the Sewerage and Water Board, which was responsible for keeping up the drainage canals in the neighborhood [*see below*].

5. For a more extensive overview of the changes in demographics, see Juliette Landphair's "'The Forgotten People of New Orleans': Community, Vulnerability, and the Lower Ninth Ward" in the *Journal of American History* December 2007: 837–845.

6. For great maps and a discussion of the impact of topography on the growth of the city, see Richard Campanella's 2002 *Time and Place in New Orleans: Past Geographies in the Present Day*. Gretna: Pelican Publishing Company: 45–61.

7. Craig Colten 2005 *Unnatural Metropolis: Wresting New Orleans from Nature*. Baton Rouge: Louisiana State University Press: 100–107.

8. In his short photo essay from 1980, "Men and Buildings: American Victoriana," Clarence John Laughlin writes, "This extraordinary eight-sided house was built in 1905 by Capt. Milton Doullut 'with his own hands and the help of his son and one negro.' It is crowned with the replica of a pilot house from which, after his retirement from the river, Capt. Doullut could watch the Mississippi River and its boats, both of which he loved. The slim columns of its encircling gallery (modeled after a steam–boat's decks) are enwreathed with swags of wooden balls, which move in the wind to suggest the feeling of the building moves like a boat!" *Perspecta* 17: 85.

9. Claude F. Jacobs and Andrew J. Kaslow 2001 *The Spiritual Churches of New Orleans: Origins, Beliefs and Rituals of an African American Religion*. Knoxville: University of Tenessee Press: 38.

10. This excerpt comes from Elizabeth Cousins Rogers' document, "Riding the Nightmare Express," which is mostly about her experiences during Hurricane Betsy. An outspoken antiracist advocate, she detailed the discrimination her Black neighbors faced after the flooding of the Lower Ninth Ward. The full document can be downloaded at the Hurricane Digital Memory Bank, an important archive developed after Katrina by a group of history professors from around the country: http://www.hurricanearchive.org/object/26649.

11. Jacobs and Kaslow 2001: 40.

12. Campanella 2002: 73–78.

13. Quoted from "Notes on the Lower Ninth Ward," in *War Outside My Window: Dispatches from New Orleans Youth*, a collection of student writings and photography from John McDonogh Senior High, McDonogh 35 (where Javon was a student), and the New Orleans Center for Creative Arts, edited by Rachel Breunlin and Michel Varisco.

14. Campanella 2002: 78.

15. See John Barry 1997 *Rising Tide: How the Great Mississippi Flood of 1927 Changed America*. New York: Touchstone. He writes of the New Orleans elite, many of whom were members of the exclusive carnival organization, the Boston Club: "The fine families, as if on picnic, traveled down to see the great explosion that would send dirt hundreds of feet and create a sudden Niagara Falls...But not just anyone could witness the explosion. It required an official permit. The men who decided to dynamite the levee controlled those permits. Residents of St. Bernard could not witness the destruction of the levee, and their parish" (256).

16. See Elizabeth Cotton Rogers' "Riding the Nightmare Express." Also, Kathy Randel's Artspot Production, "Lower 9 Stories," which includes oral histories of residents talking about their belief that the Industrial Canal was dynamited during Hurricane Betsy: http://www.artspotproductions.org/past_low9.htm. Accessed on November 30, 2008.

For a recount of the discourses around levee dynamiting during Hurricane Katrina, see "'They' Destroyed New Orleans" by Kenneth Cooper, posted on AlterNet's website on December 24, 2005, as well as the comments that follow: http://www.alternet.org/katrina/30044/%27they%27_destroyed_new_orleans/?page=1.

The opinion of Cooper's cousin, Kenneth, is representative of the conspiracy theory. Cooper writes, "Like everyone else in my family, [Kenneth] lost everything when Hurricane Katrina hit New Orleans. Now he sits in my driveway on a Saturday night in LaPlace...trying to understand why...'Them people blew them levees... They wanted to save the white people Uptown.'" As the majority of members on the Mississippi River Commission, which was responsible for the St. Bernard river levee being dynamited in 1927, were a part of the American "uptown" sector of carnival krewes and exclusive social clubs, Kenneth's assertion are informed by a historical precedent.

17. Landphair 2007: 840.

18. Aesha Rasheed 2007 "Education in New Orleans: Some Background" in *High School Journal* 90.2: 4–7.

19. Rasheed 2006; Landphair 2007.

20. Landphair 2007: 842.

21. Sutton 2005: 37.

22. Edna Gundersen's "Fats Domino: Alive and Kickin'" published in *USA Today* on September 23, 2007.

23. See Joyce Jackson's 2005 "Declaration of Taking Twice: The Fazendeville Community of the Lower Ninth Ward" and Allison Pena's "Wade in the Water" in *American Anthropologist* 108 (4):765–798.

24. The planning that caused the most backlash from residents was the Urban Land Institute's preliminary report to Mayor Ray Nagin's Bring New Orleans Back committee in November of 2005. Composed of 50 experts in urban and post disaster planning, it was created without the input of residents of the city.

Martha Carr's "Rebuilding Should Begin on High Ground, Group Says," published in *The Times-Picayune* on November 19, 2005, outlines the most controversial recommendations: "In the most comprehensive recovery plan proposed to date, a panel...said New Orleans should concentrate its rebuilding efforts on the sections of the city that occupy the high ground, while securing lower-lying areas for potential long-term rebirth...

"The group went so far as to draft a color-coded map of the city showing three 'investment zones' the city may want to follow. The first zone included the high parts of the city, like Uptown and the French Quarter, which panelists say is ready for rehabilitation immediately. The second zone highlighted the mid-ground, which the panel suggested is also ready for individual rehabilitation, with some opportunities to put together parcels of land for green space or redevelopment.

"The last zone, which included some of the city's hardest hit neighborhoods, needs additional study, but could have the potential for mass buyouts and future green space, the panel said. Those areas include most of eastern New Orleans east and Gentilly; the northern part of Lakeview; and parts of the Lower 9th Ward, Broadmoor, Mid-City and Hollygrove."

25. See NOLAplans' website at http://www.nola-plans.com/timeline/ for a comprehensive look at the recovery planning in New Orleans since Hurricane Katrina. The site has links to numerous articles about the rebuilding process.

26. There is a useful demographic chart in Rebekah Green, Lisa K. Bates, and Andrew Smyth's 2007 "Impediments to Recovery in New Orleans' Upper and Lower Ninth Ward: One Year after Hurricane Katrina" in *Disasters* 31(4):314.

27. Green, Bates, and Smyth 2007: 327–328.

28. Deborah Sontag "When the Lower Ninth Posed Proudly" published in *The New York Times* on February 9, 2006.

29. Rebecca Solnit "The Lower Ninth Battles Back" in *The Nation*. September 10, 2007: 14.

30. All of the Lower Ninth Ward organizations mentioned have websites where project and contact information can be found.

31. For more information about the performances as well as the coalitions built around Paul Chan's *Waiting for Godot*, see Billy Sothern's "Waiting for Godot in a Wasteland" in *The Nation* December 31, 2007: 25-26

and Sally Heller's "Godot in the Crescent City" in *Art in America* Feb 2008: 43-45. Other information about the productions come from conversations with Paul and the Neighborhood Story Project's experience as one of the "community partners."

32. Many of Prospect.1's art installations were housed in neighborhood spaces, such as the Battle Ground Baptist Church, Keith Calhoun and Chandra McCormick's L9 Gallery, and the the Lower Ninth Village. Others, like Artist Mark Bradford's ark, were locatd on an empty lots. "Mirtha" was built on the the 2200 block of Caffin Avenue. For more information about the Biennial, see its 2008 catalogue, *Prospect.1* New Orleans. Brooklyn: Picturebox.

"Mirtha." Photograph by Rachel Breunlin.

33. See Kalamu ya Salaam's discussion of the song in his essay, "LIL' RASCALS BRASS BAND / "Knock With Me—Rock With Me" at http://www.kalamu.com/bol/2008/06/02/lil'-rascals-brass-band-"knock-with-me---rock-with-me"/ Accessed November 28, 2008.

Part III: Mardi Gras Indians

Ronald's narratives are based on edited interviews conducted by Rachel Breunlin from January 2007–November of 2008. Other quotations come from interviews conducted by Rachel, except for those with Monk Boudreaux, Keith "Kiki" Gibson, and Victor Harris, which were edited from interviews by Lindsey Darnell.

1. Robert Farris Thompson 1979 *African Art in Motion*. Berkeley, CA: University of California Press: XII.

2. Jelly Roll Morton Complete Library Of Congress Recordings by Alan Lomax.

3. See Roach 1992 "Mardi Gras Indians and Others: Genealogies of American Performance" in *Theatre Journal* 44 (4): 461. Also, George Lipsitz's 1988 "Mardi Gras Indians: Carnival and Counter-Narrative in Black New Orleans" in *Cultural Critique* 10: 102.

4. Kalamu ya Salaam 1997 "Introduction" in *He's the Prettiest: A Tribute to Big Chief Allison "Tootie" Montana's 50 Years of Mardi Gras Indian Suiting* published by New Orleans Museum of Art: 11–12. For more on race and carnival in New Orleans, see James Gill's 1997 *Lords of Misrule: Mardi Gras and the Politics of Race in New Orleans*, published by University Press of Mississippi; John M. Barry's 1998 *Rising Tide: The Great Mississippi Flood of 1927 and How It Changed America*, published by Simon & Schuster; and Rebecca Snedeker's 2006 documentary film *By Invitation Only* from New Day Films.

5. The Buechel Memorial Lakota Museum is the result of the collecting efforts of Fr. Eugene Buechel, S.J., a Jesuit Catholic priest who worked among the Lakota for most of his life and was a student of their language and culture. The museum is unique in that the collection never left the Rosebud reservation in South Dakota but remains there where Native people have access. For more information, see their website: http://www.sfmission.org/museum/.

6. Robert Farris Thompson 1988 "Recapturing Heaven's Glamour: Afro-Caribbean Festivalizing Arts" in *Caribbean Festival Arts: Each and Every Bit of Difference*, edited by John W. Nunley and Judith Bettelheim. Seattle: University of Washington Press: 25.

7. Smith 1994.

8. Personal communication with Lil Walter Cook, who is working on an extensive history of his tribe, the Creole Wild West.

9. Jerry Brock 1989 "The Indians" *Wavelength* 101:17-20.

10. *Tootie's Last Suit* 2004, directed by Lisa Katzman.

11. When journalist David Kunian visited Monk Boudreaux, Big Chief of the Golden Eagles, he was shown a book, *The American Indian: Special Edition for Young Readers*, by Oliver LaFarge that includes a painting dated 1735. Kunian describes the scene featuring "several Choctaw Indians standing around a campsite in Louisiana. Standing with them is a similarly dressed African American boy." See Kunian's article in the *Gambit Weekly* on February 21 2006.

12. Jeffrey David Ehrenreich 2004 "Bodies, Beads, Bones, and Feathers: The Masking Tradition of Mardi Gras Indians in New Orleans—A Photo Essay" in *City & Society* 16 (1): 148.

13. The Backstreet Cultural Museum's website: http://www.backstreetmuseum.org/NEA_release.pdf has more information about the 2007 National Endowment for the Arts' funded cultural exchange. White Buffalo Day in New Orleans was organized in 1996 by Reverend Goat Carson. That year, Arvol Looking Horse, the 19th Generation Keeper of the Sacred White Buffalo Calf Pipe amongst the Lakota, was given the key to the city by Mayor Marc Morial and August 27th was declared "White Buffalo Day." In 2000, Chief Looking Horse and Reverend Carson were featured on John Sinclair and His Blues Scholars' White Buffalo Prayer, released by SpyBoy Records.

14. In 1987, Allison "Tootie" Montana was named a National Endowment for the Arts Heritage Fellow. The NEA has since supported Mardi Gras Indian art in New Orleans in a number of capacities. In addition to its work with the Backstreet Cultural Museum, it has also supported Xavier University Community Arts program's "Mardi Gras Indian Arts Intensive"—a summer arts program for youth ages 11–14 that focuses on the art and culture of the sewing traditions. Big Chiefs Darryl Montana and Larry Bannock were hired to run the workshops.

15. William Fagaly 1997 "Introduction" to *He's the Prettiest: A Tribute to Big Chief Allison "Tootie" Montana's 50 years of Mardi Gras Indian Suiting*. New Orleans: New Orleans Museum of Art: 7.

16. Henry John Drewal and John Mason 1998 *Beads, Body, and Soul: Art and Light in the Yoruba Universe*. Los Angeles: UCLA Fowler Museum of Cultural History: 39.

17. Ibid: 39.

18. Ibid: 54.

19. Information on Plains Indian beading comes from the 2005 catalogue *Blue Winds Dancing: The Whitecloud Collection of Native American Art*. New Orleans: New Orleans Museum of Art: 87.

20. Elizabeth McAlister's 2002 R*ara! Vodou, Power, and Performance in Haiti and its Diaspora*. Berkeley: University of California Press.

21. Susan Elizabeth Tselos 1996 "Threads of Reflection: Costumes of Haitian Rara." *African Arts* XXIX (Spring 1996): 58–65.

22. Helene Bellour and Samuel Kisner 1998 "Amerindian Masking in Trinidad's Carnival: The House of Black Elk in San Fernando" in *The Drama Review* 42 (3): 147–168.

23. Rosita M. Sands 1991 "Carnival Celebrations in Africa and the New World: Junkanoo and the Black Indians of Mardi Gras" in *Black Music Research Journal* 11 (1): 90.

24. Roach 1992: 463; also Lipsitz 1998: 105–114.

25. For more information on carnival groups in Haiti, see Gage Averill's 1994 "Anraje to Angaje: Carnival Politics and Music in Haiti" in *Ethnomusicology* 38(2):220–247. For more on Rara costumes, see Delores Yonker's "Rara in Haiti" in Nunley and Bettelheim 1988 and Tselos 1996.

26. Ehrenreich 2004: 117.

27. For more on the relationship between the Seventh Ward building crafts and Mardi Gras Indian designs, see Nick Spitzer's 2002 "The Aesthetics of Work and Play in Creole New Orleans" in *Raised to the Trade: Creole Building Arts of New Orleans*, edited by John Ethan Hankins and Steven Maklansky. New Orleans: New Orleans Museum of Art: 96-130. Below is a photograph of Joyce Montana, Tootie Montana's wife, pointing to a plaster face of an Indian he made on the front of their house in the Seventh Ward.

Photograph by Rachel Breunlin.

27. Drewal and Mason 1998: 54.

28. This section was inspired by interviews Ronald had with Katy Reckdahl for her article "Innovations Cause

Controversy Among Mardi Gras Indians" published in *The Times-Picayune* on May 26, 2007.

Part IV: Social Aid & Pleasure Clubs

A portion of the introductory essay was first published in 1999 as "Second Lines, Minstrelsy, and the Contested Landscapes of New Orleans' Afro-Creole Festivals" in the journal *Cultural Anthropology*. 14(4):472-504.

Ronald's narratives are edited from interviews conducted by Rachel Breunlin and Helen Regis in the fall of 2008. Other quotations come from interviews conducted by Rachel, except for those with from Lois Andrews, Linda Porter, Adrian "Coach Teedy" Gaddies, Kevin Dunn, and Jack Matranga, which were edited from interviews by Lindsey Darnell. Joe Stern's contribution, a written reflection on Kemp's, was coordinated by Lea Downing.

1. Paul Gilroy 1993 *Small Acts: Thoughts on the Politics of Black Cultures*. New York: Serpent's Tail: 42.

2. Rafael Brea and José Millet 2001 "Glossary of Popular Festivals" in *Cuban Festivals: A Century of Afro-Cuban Culture*, edited by Judith Bettelheim. Princeton: Marcus Weiner Publishers: 177.

3. The history of these organizations is told in Claude Francis Jacobs 1980 *Strategies of Neighborhood Health-Care Among New Orleans Blacks: From Voluntary Associations to Public Policy*. Ph.D. Dissertation, Department of Anthropology, Tulane University. Also, Harry J. Walker 1936 *Negro Benevolent Societies in New Orleans: A Study of Their Structure, Function, and Membership*. Nashville: Department of Social Science, Fisk University.

4. Records for the Girod Street Cemetery (uptown and mostly Protestant) and Saint Louis Number Two (downtown and mostly Catholic) show that approximately 200 black benevolent societies had built tombs during the 19th century in these two burial grounds alone.

5. Jacobs 1980:88–89; also Walker 1936:34–35.

6. Eric Arnesen 1994 *Waterfront Workers of New Orleans: Race, Class, and Politics, 1863–1923.* Chicago: University of Illinois Press: 50. Previously published in 1991 in a cloth edition by Oxfor University Press.

7. Arnesen 1994: 9.

8. Jacobs 1980:91.

9. Historian Caryn Cossé Bell recounts, "After Napoleon sold the colony to the United States in 1803, American officials were…alarmed by the spectacle of armed free black milita units and the aggressive actions of free men of color in demanding their rights…The appearance of the black corps on parade at the formal ceremonies in December [1803] thoroughly frightened white officials." Carolyn Cossé Bell 1997 *Revolution, Romanticism, and the Afro-Creole Protest tradition in Louisiana, 1718–1868.* Baton Rouge: Louisiana State University Press: 29.

10. Philip S. Foner 1950 *The Life and Writings of Frederick Douglas Vol. 2.* New York: International Publishers.

11. Genevieve Fabre 1994 "African-American Commemorative Celebrations in the Nineteenth Century" in *History and Memory in African-American Culture.* Geneviève Fabre and Robert O¹Meally, eds. New York: Oxford University Press: 72–91.

12. Fabre 1994:87.

13. Rebecca J. Scott 2005 *Degrees of Freedom: Louisiana and Cuba After Slavery.* Cambridge: Harvard University Press: 89.

14. Herbert M. Cole's 1975 "The Art of Festival in Ghana" in *African Arts* 8 (3): 12.

15. For more information on Cuba, see Bettelheim 2001. On Haiti, see Elizabeth McAlister 2002 and Averill 1994.

16. CubaNOLA Arts Collective text panels from "Santiago de Cuba: ReBirth & Congas en la Calle," a photography exhibit at the McKenna Museum of African American Art, January 5 to February 23, 2008.

17. McAlister 2002: 178. See her website, "Rara: Vodou, Power, and Performance in Haiti and Its Diaspora," for more on the processions: http://rara.wesleyan.edu/.

18. Ronald is referencing the Ninth Ward second lining history documented in Nine Times Social and Pleasure Club's 2006 *Coming Out the Door for the Ninth Ward.* New Orleans: Neighborhood Story Project.

19. For more on the role of jazz funerals in New Orleans, see Helen Regis' "Blackness and the Politics of Memory in the New Orleans Second line" in *American Ethnologist* 28(4): 757–777.

20. Kalamu ya Salaam's "LIL' RASCALS BRASS BAND / "Knock With Me – Rock With Me" again at http://www.kalamu.com/bol/2008/06/02/lil'-rascals-brass-band-"knock-with-me-–-rock-with-me"/.

21. For more on the use of umbrellas in West Africa, see Cole 1975 as well as his photograph from Ghana below:

22. Listen to "Wipe Me Down" on Lil' Boosie's 2007 *Survival of the Fittest* released on Asylum Records.

23. Listen to "We Fly High" on Jim Jones' 2006 *Hustler's POME (Product of My Environment)* released on Koch Records.

24. Marcyliena Morgan 2005 "After...Word!" in *Hip Hop Philosophy: rhyme 2 reason*, edited by Derrick Darby and Tommie Shelby. Chicago: Open Court Publishing Company.

Part V: Skull & Bones

1. We are indebted to Royce Osborn and his film *All on a Mardi Gras Day* for providing the background on Skeletons in New Orleans. His film is quoted at length here and throughout the introductory essay. For more information about the film and to purchase a DVD: www.spyboypics.com. All quotations from Royce in Part V come from a talk he gave at the Prytania Theatre on October 29, 2007 for the Young Leadership Council's "One Book, One New Orleans" reading campaign, co-sponsored by the Neighborhood Story Project. The full talk can be downloaded at: http://neighborhoodstoryproject.org/walkin.html.

Quotations by Derek Meilleur are from interviews by Rachel Breunlin in January 2005. Ronald's narrative is from interviews conducted by Rachel Breunlin in May of 2008. Others by Brian Bush and Charles Silver were edited from interviews by Lindsey Darnell.

2. Information about the Baby Dolls comes from Helen's friendship with Miriam Reed and her participation in the 2004 revival.

3. Information about Gédé and quotations about Vodou flags comes from Tina Girouard 1994 *Sequins Artists of Haiti*. New Orleans: Contemporary Art Center. The book was published in conjunction with a two–person exhibition in 1994 of Tina and Antoine Oleyant's artwork at the CAC called "Under a Spell." A few years later, in 1998, Tina curated "Mystery and Mastery" at the CAC, which featured a wide range of Haitian artists, including sequin artists such as Antoine Oleyant, George Valris, and Edgar. A section of the exhibition was called "Links in a Cultural Chain" and featured Mardi Gras Indian suits and a drapo by Big Chief Ferdinand Birgard that is now in Andy Antippas' permanent collection [*see above*]. Thanks to Tina for numerous conversations that helped to illuminate these cross-cultural connections.

4. See *All on a Mardi Gras Day* for Bruce Barnes' full discussion.

5. Averill 1994:223.

6. Hollis "Chalkdust" Liverpool 2001 *Rituals of Power and Rebellion: The Carnival Tradition in Trinidad and Tobago, 1763–1962*. Chicago and Republic of Trinidad and Tobago: Research Associates School Times Publications/Frontline Distribution International.

7. Averill 1994: 219.

8. Charles Day, cited in Liverpool 2001: 242

9. Stanley Brandes 2006 *Skulls to the Living, Bread to the Dead: The Day of the Dead in Mexico and Beyond*. Malden, Mass.: Blackwell:52.

10. This calavera verse, printed by Antonio Vanegas Arroyo in 1905 "asserts the very egalitarian principle that Mexicans attribute to death itself." Brandes 2006:118–119.

11. Helen's thinking about performance is indebted to Margaret Drewal 1992: *Yoruba Ritual: Performance, Play, Agency*. Bloomington: Indiana University Press: 97–98.

12. Caroline W. Casey 1999 *Making the Gods Work for You: The Astrological Language of the Psyche*. New York: Three Rivers Press: 203.